Hermes Alegre
Art Gallery
By Tatay Jobo Elizes
March 2012

Welcome to Hermes Alegre Art Gallery in book form, size 8.5x11. Hermes hails from Daet, Camarines Norte and has created great excitement in the art world with his wonderful paintings for more than 20 years. He finished his Art degree from PWU in Manila. His latest art show was done in NY City in mid 2011, together with his fellow artists. The purpose of this art book is to maximize exposure of his art work. Please contact his face book account under his name in case you are interested to order his works or commission him to paint for you. Copies of this book are available online and via self-publisher. Due to his many paintings, hopefully further sequels of this book will be made. You can frame any of the paintings and hang them in walls, by buying extra copies of this book, which is very affordable.

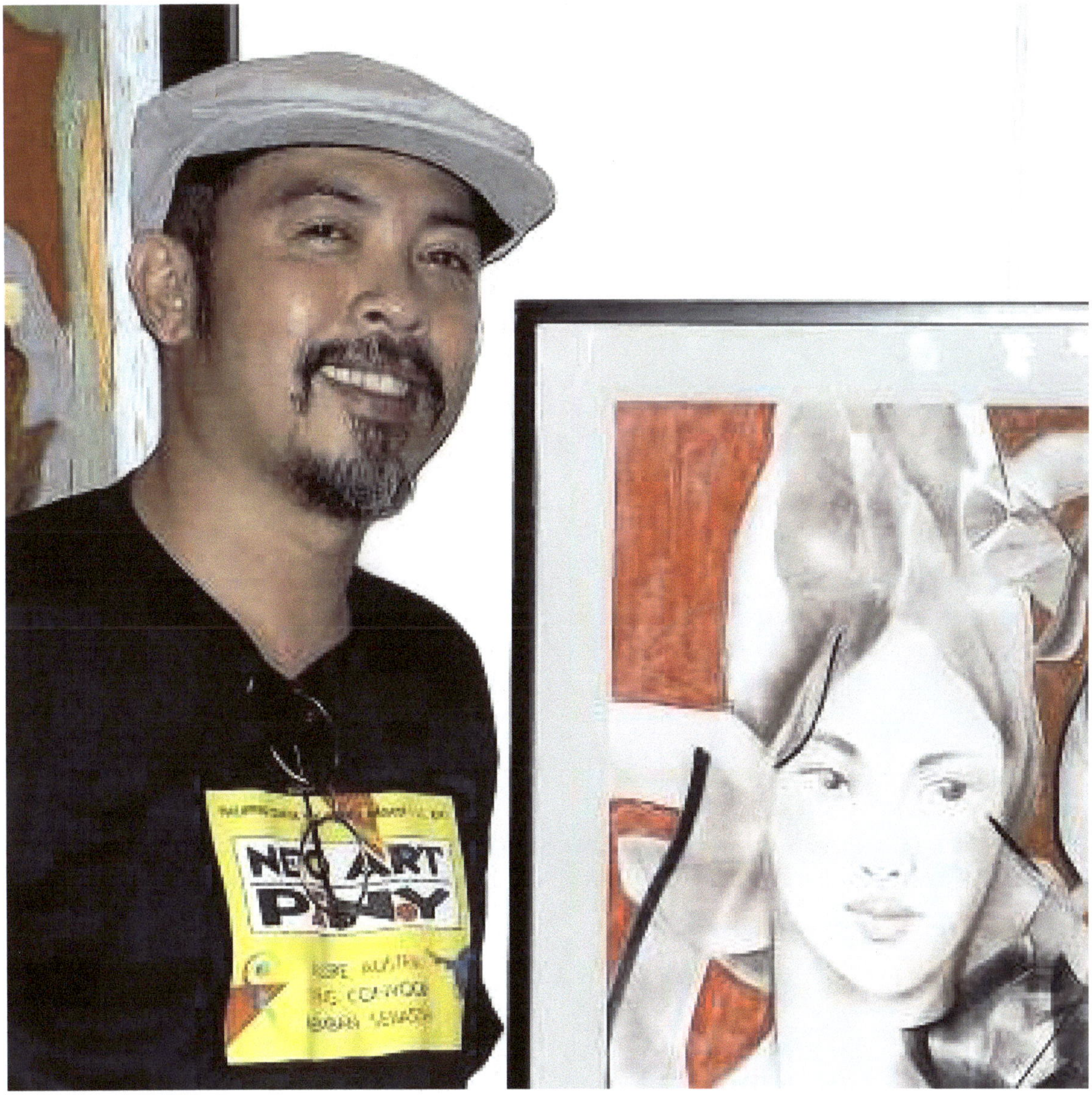

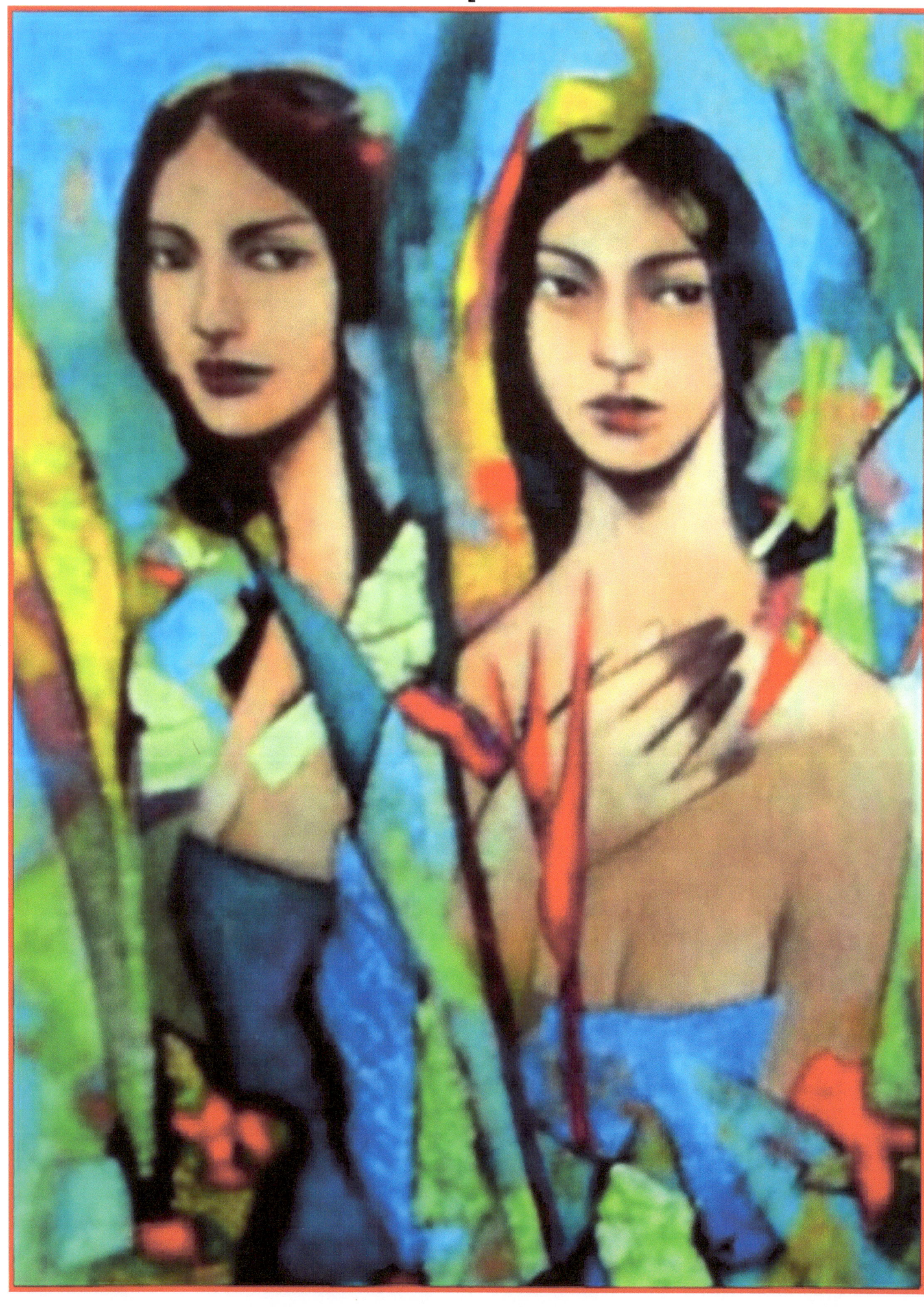

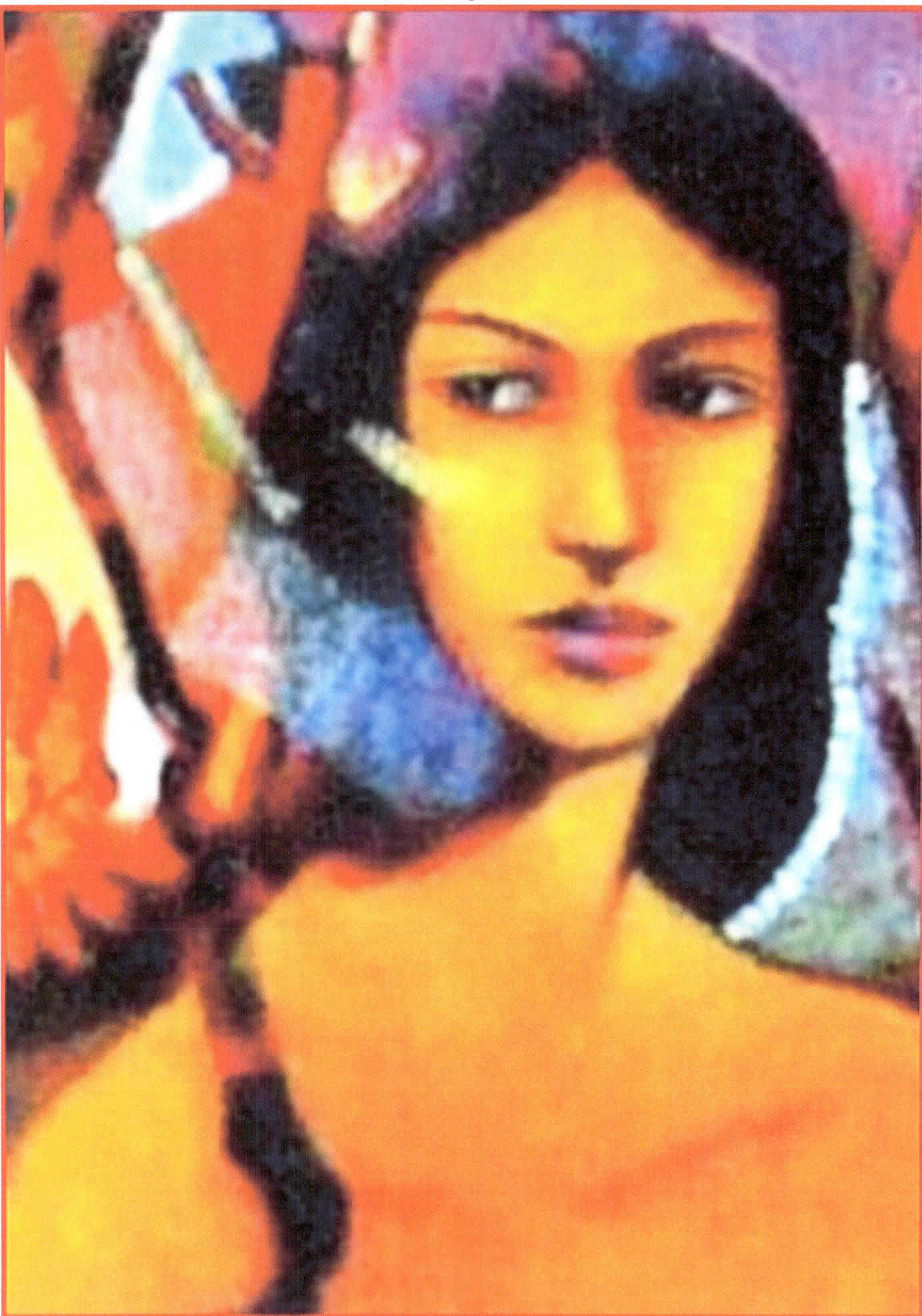

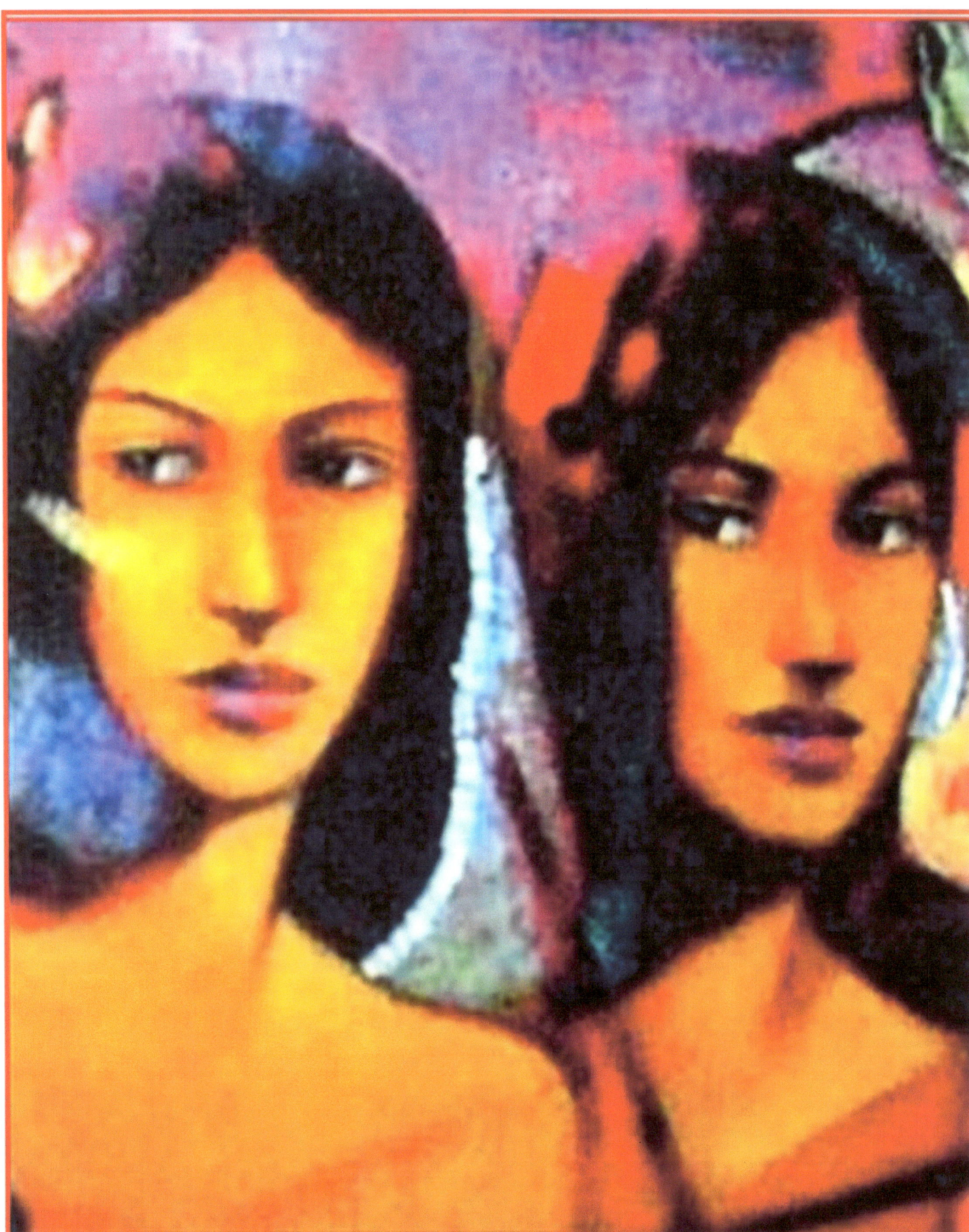

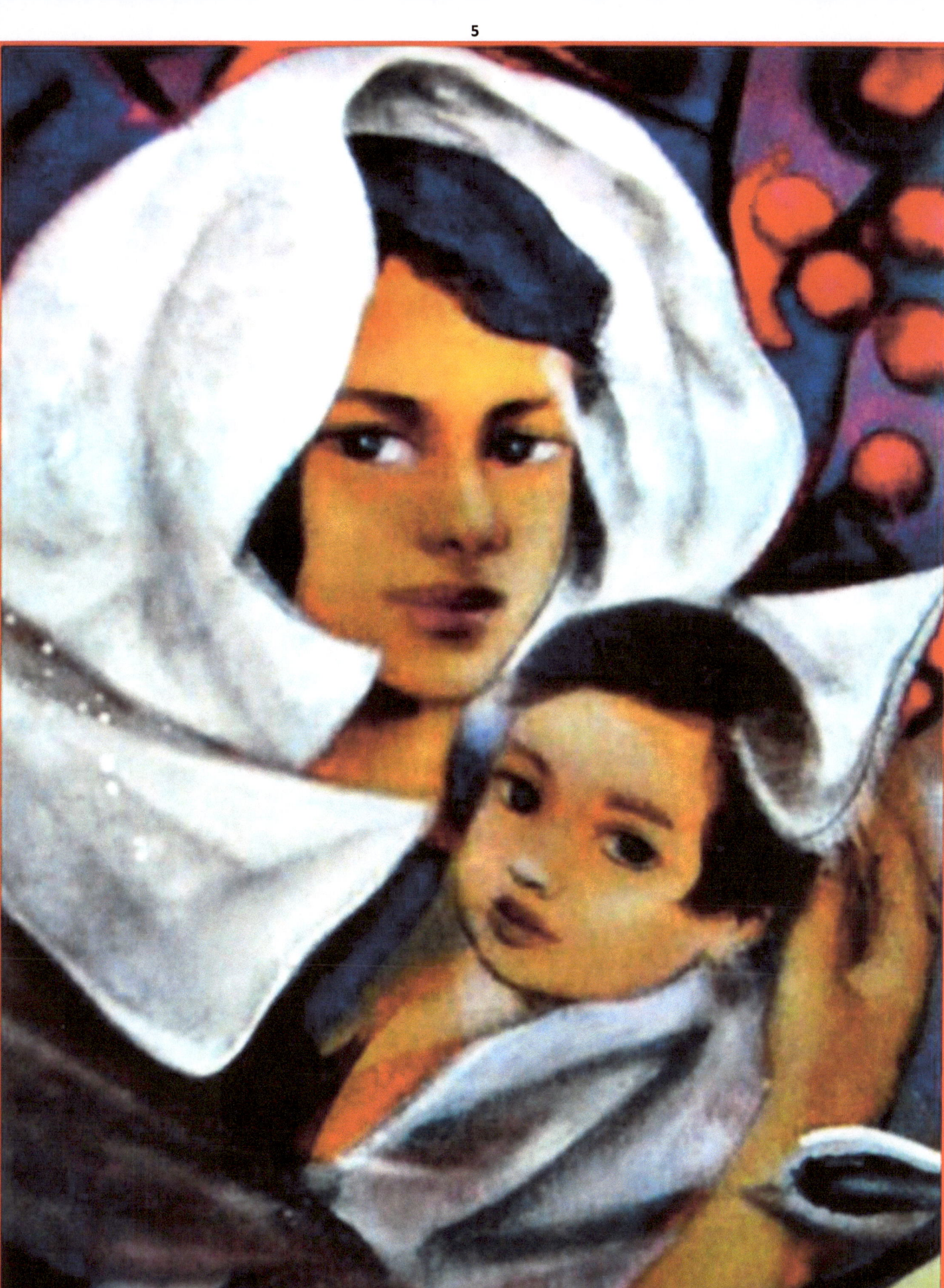

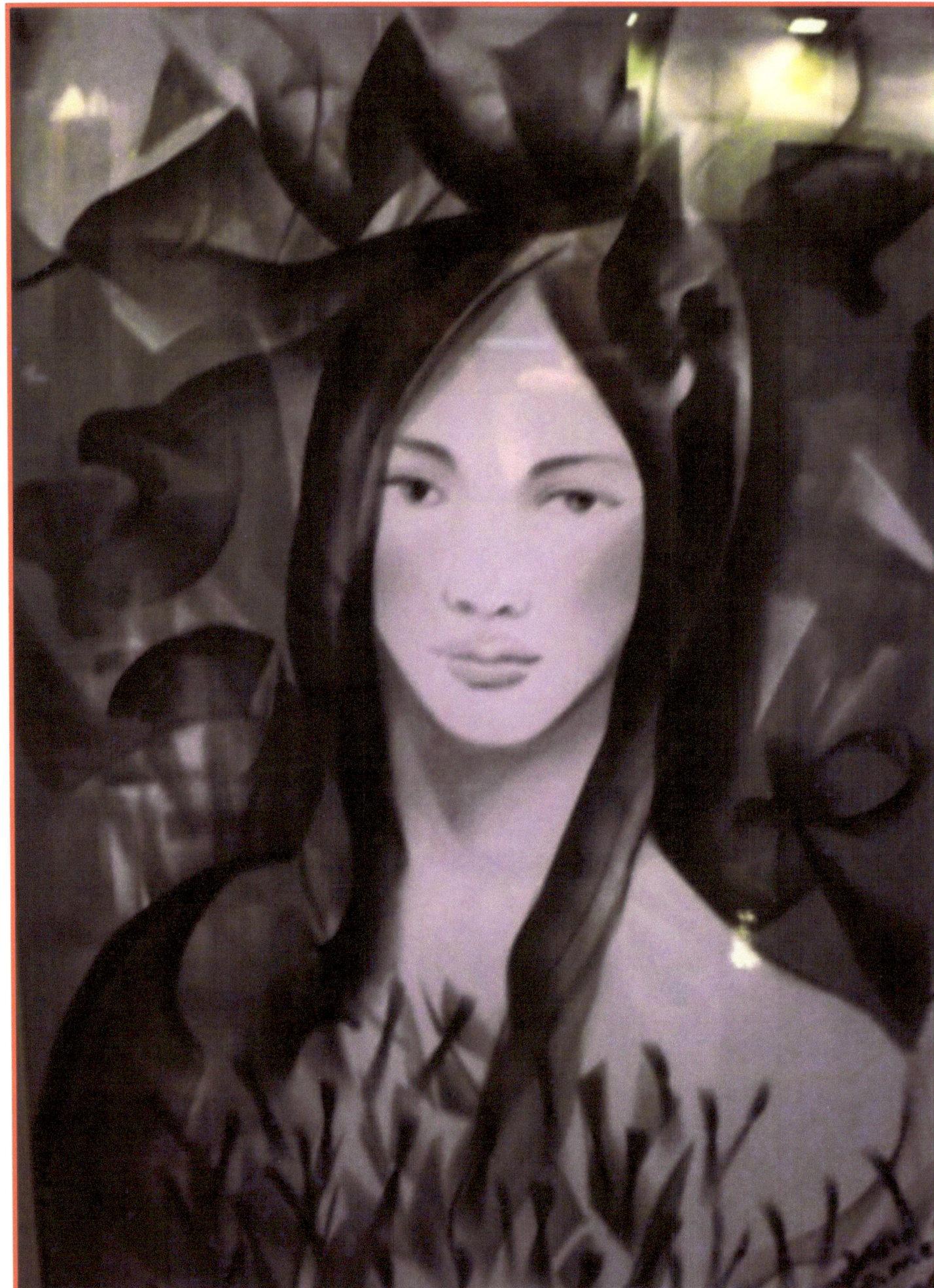

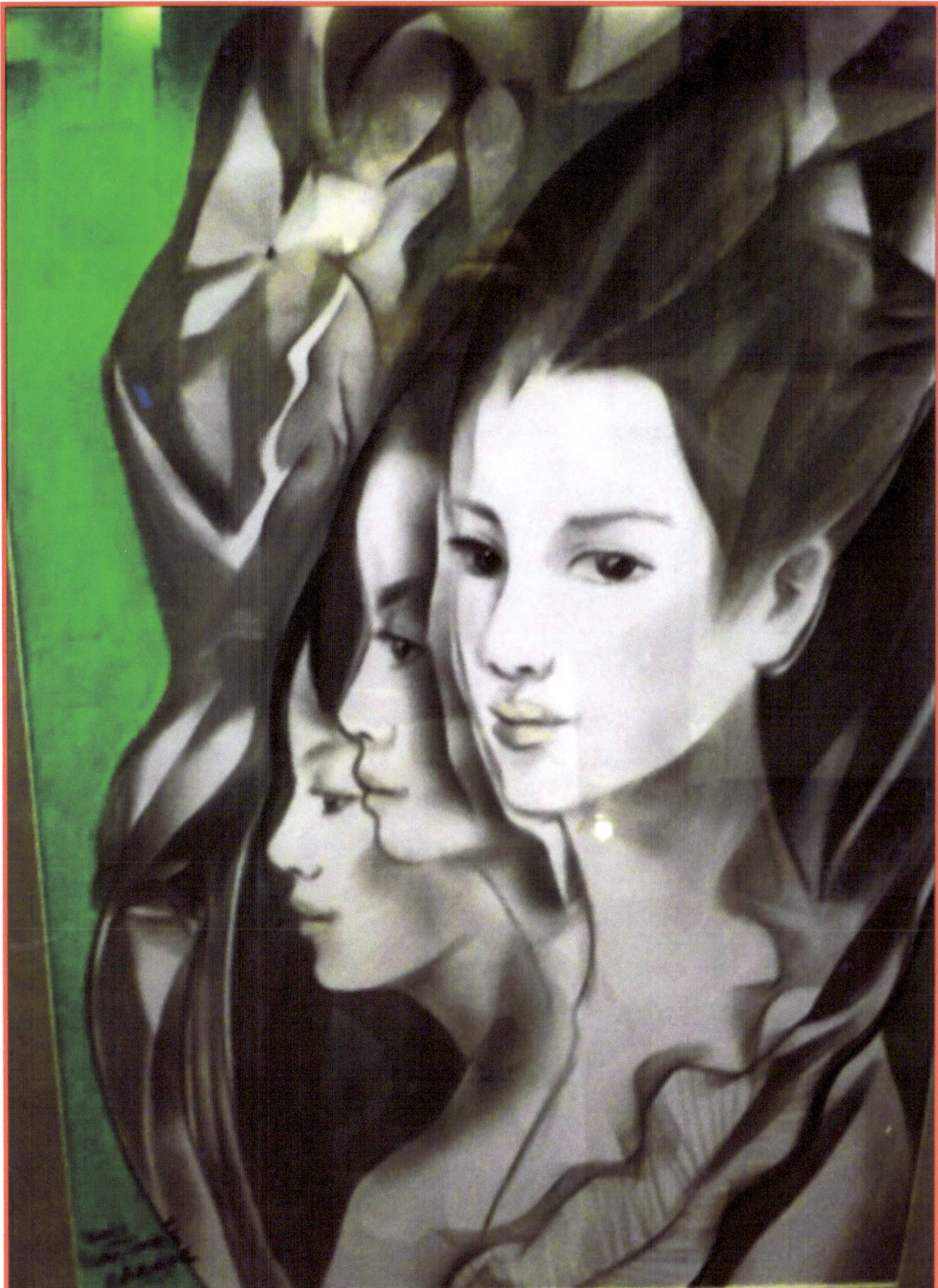

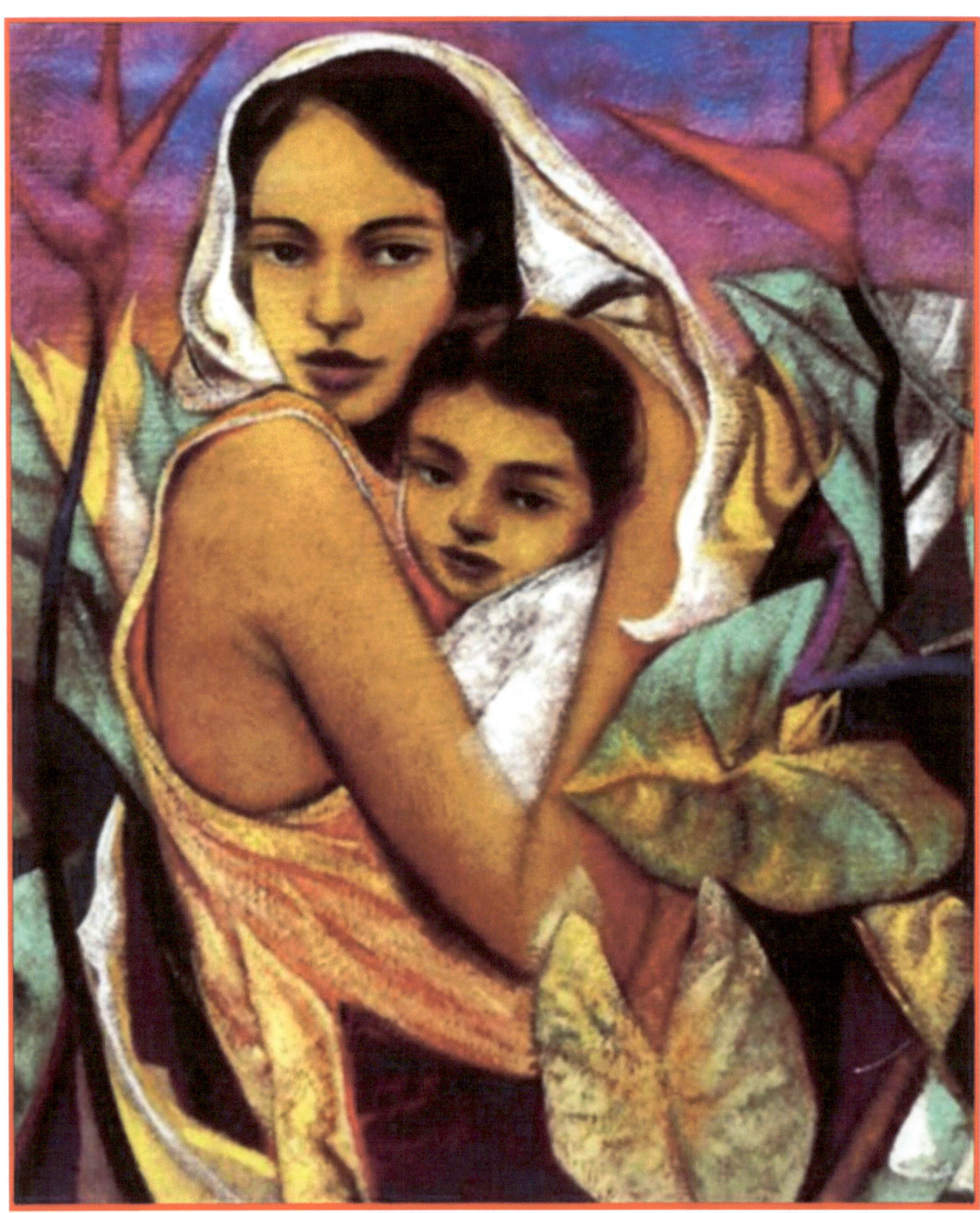

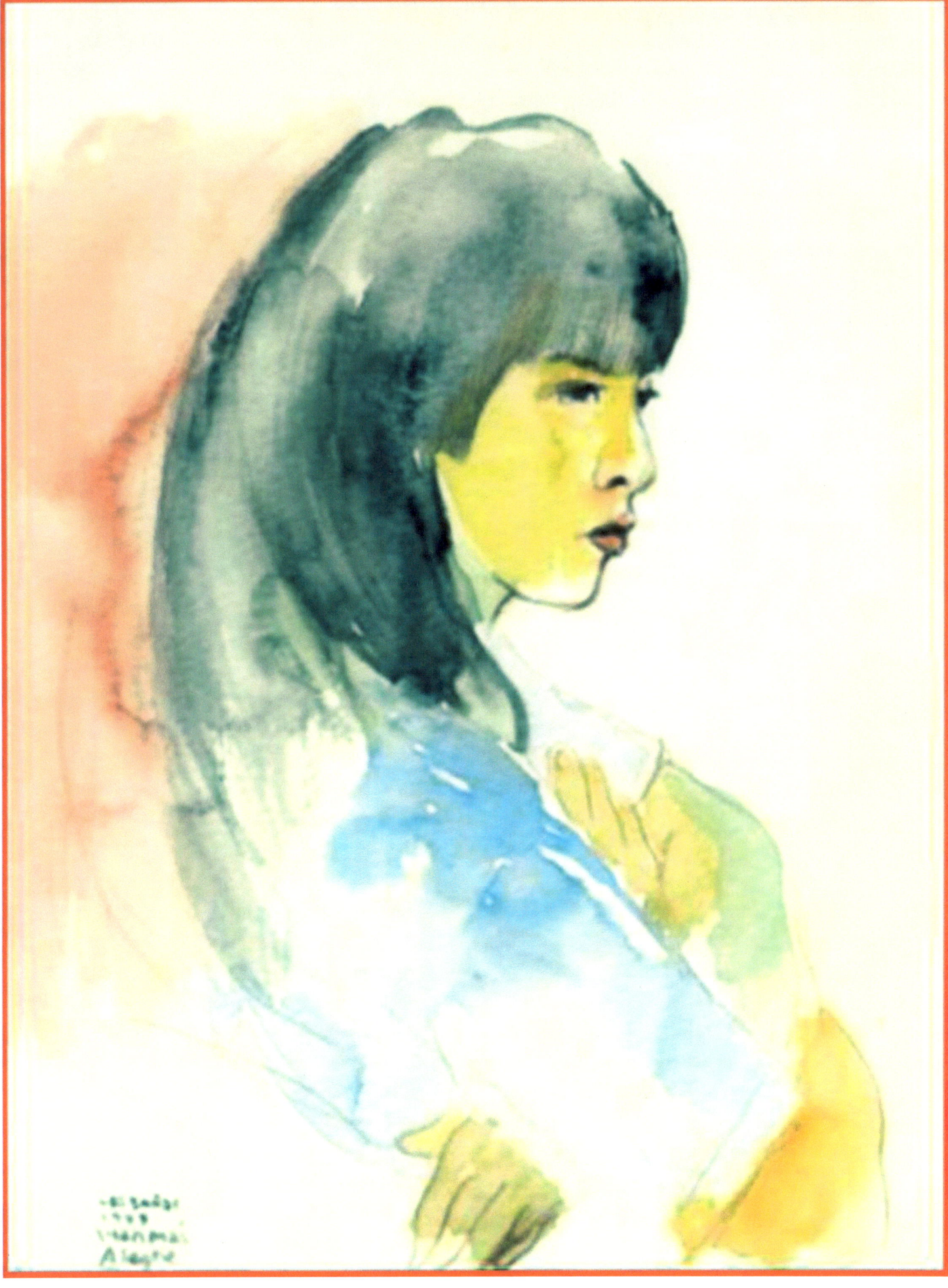

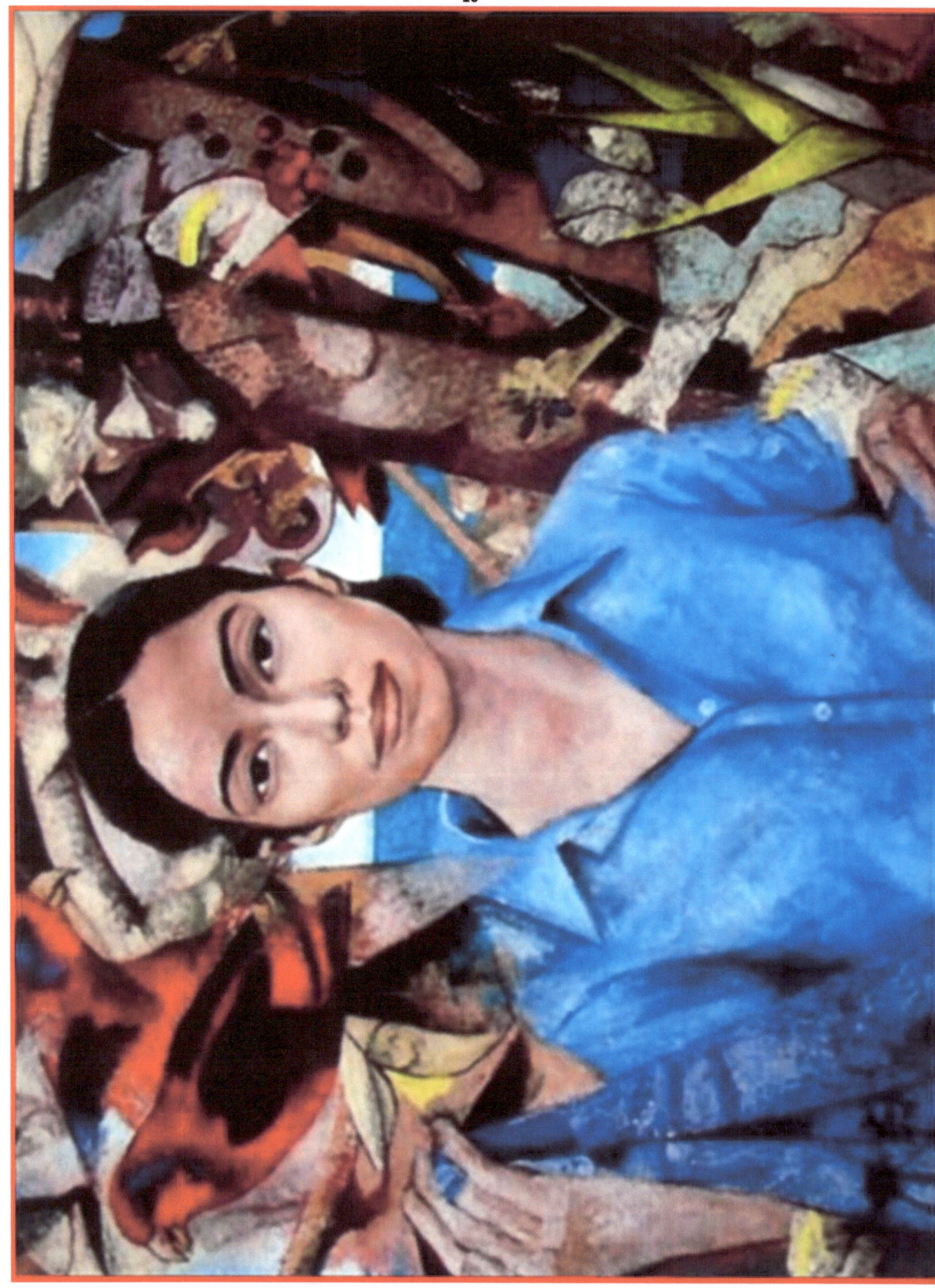

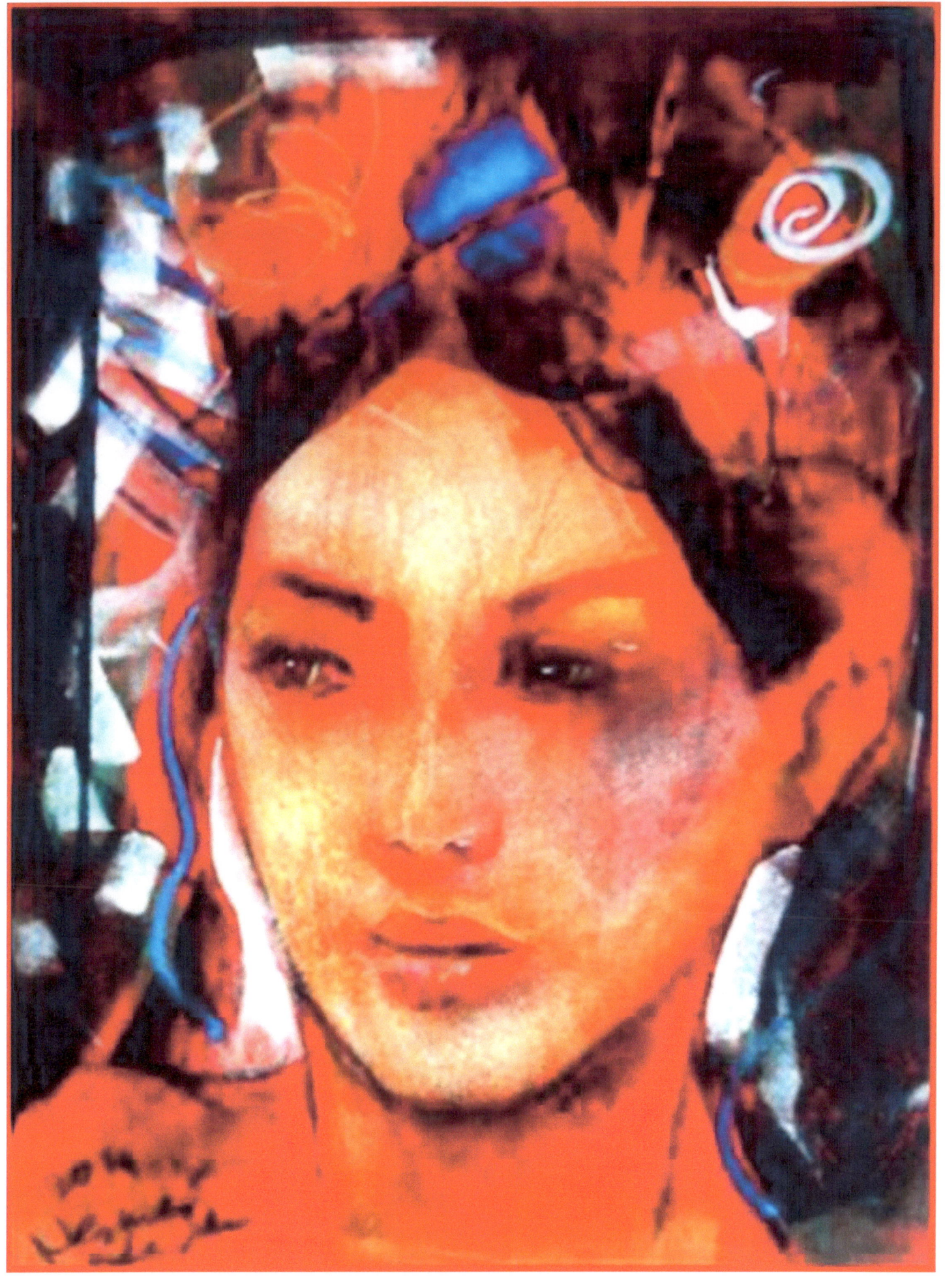

N

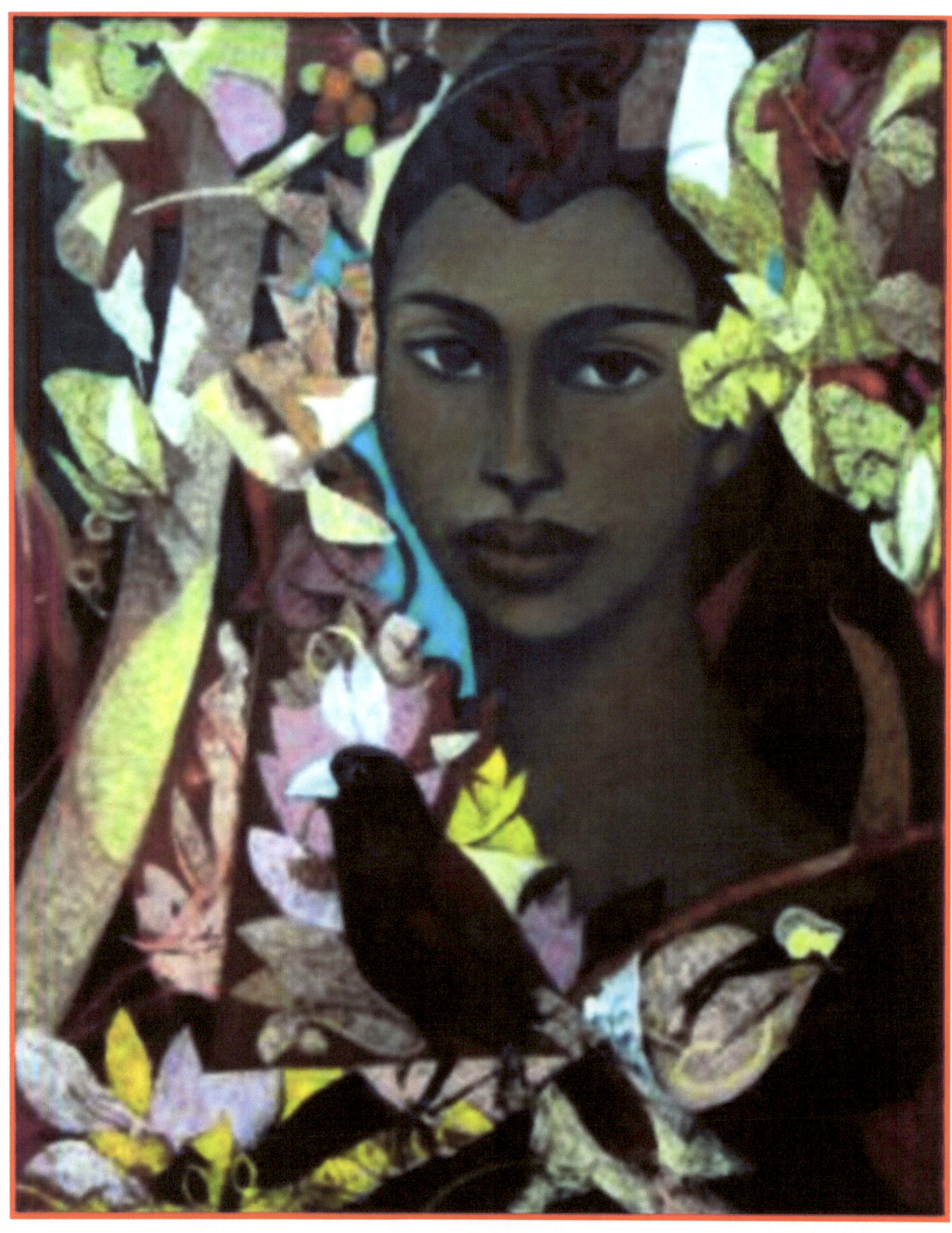

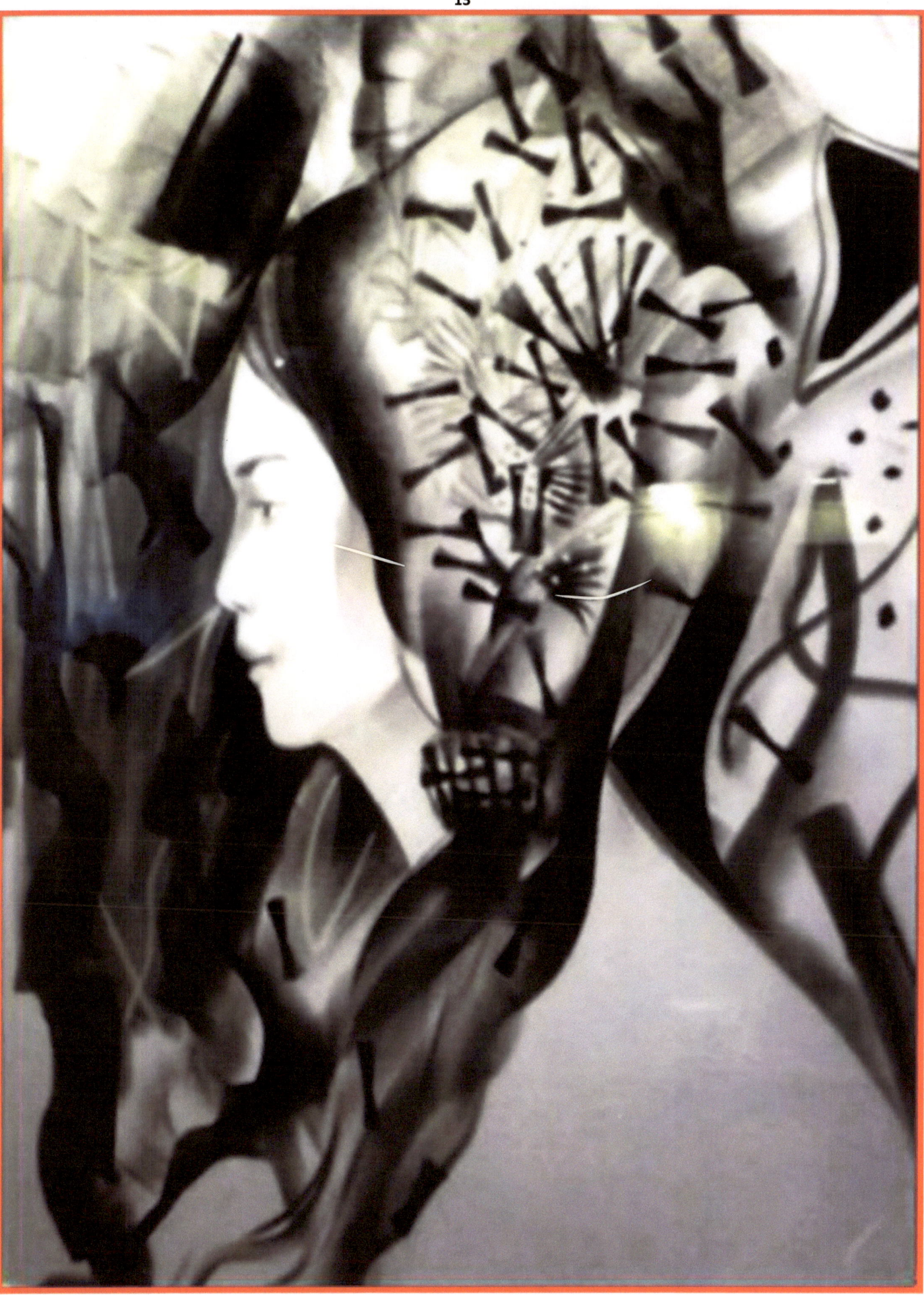

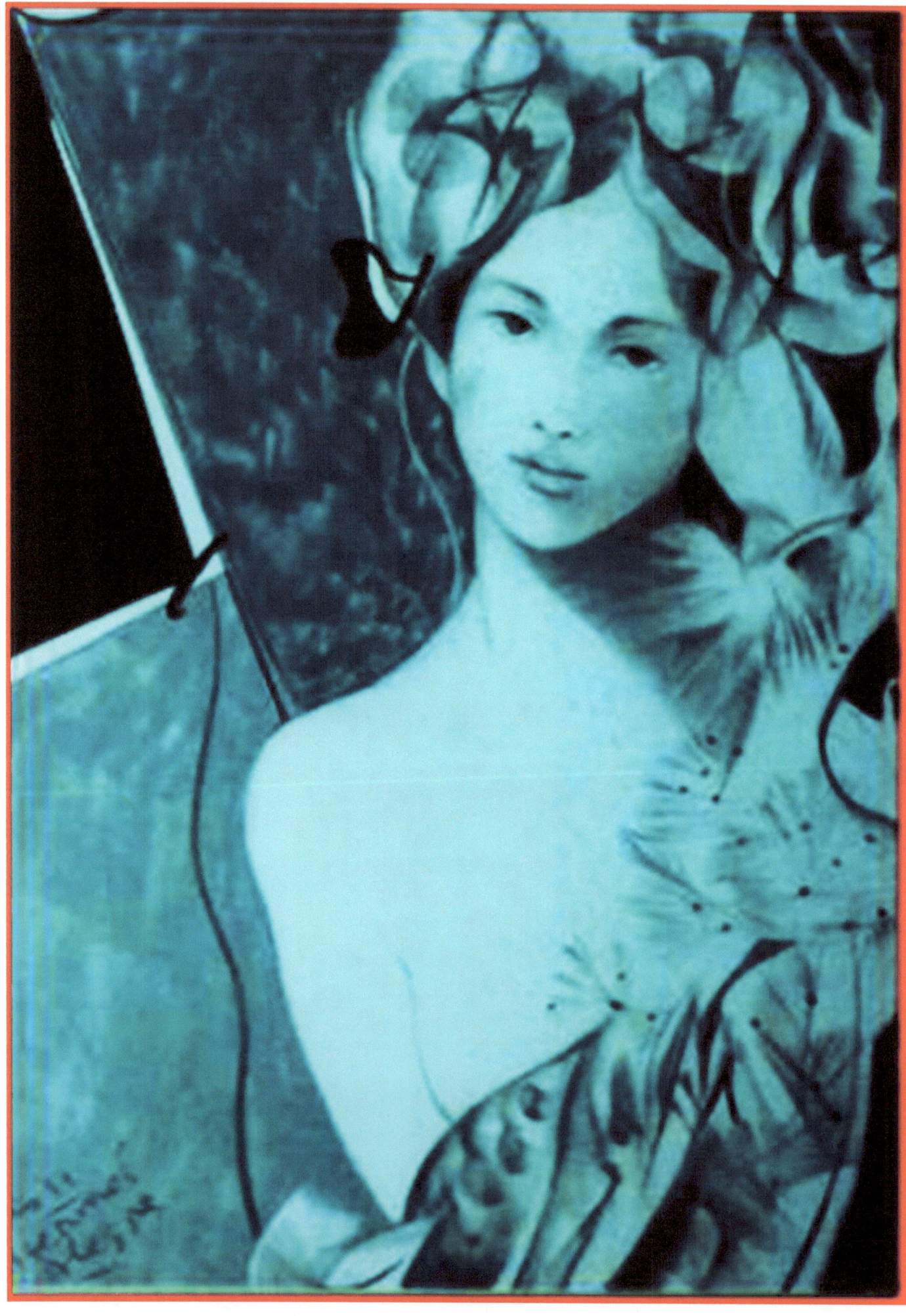

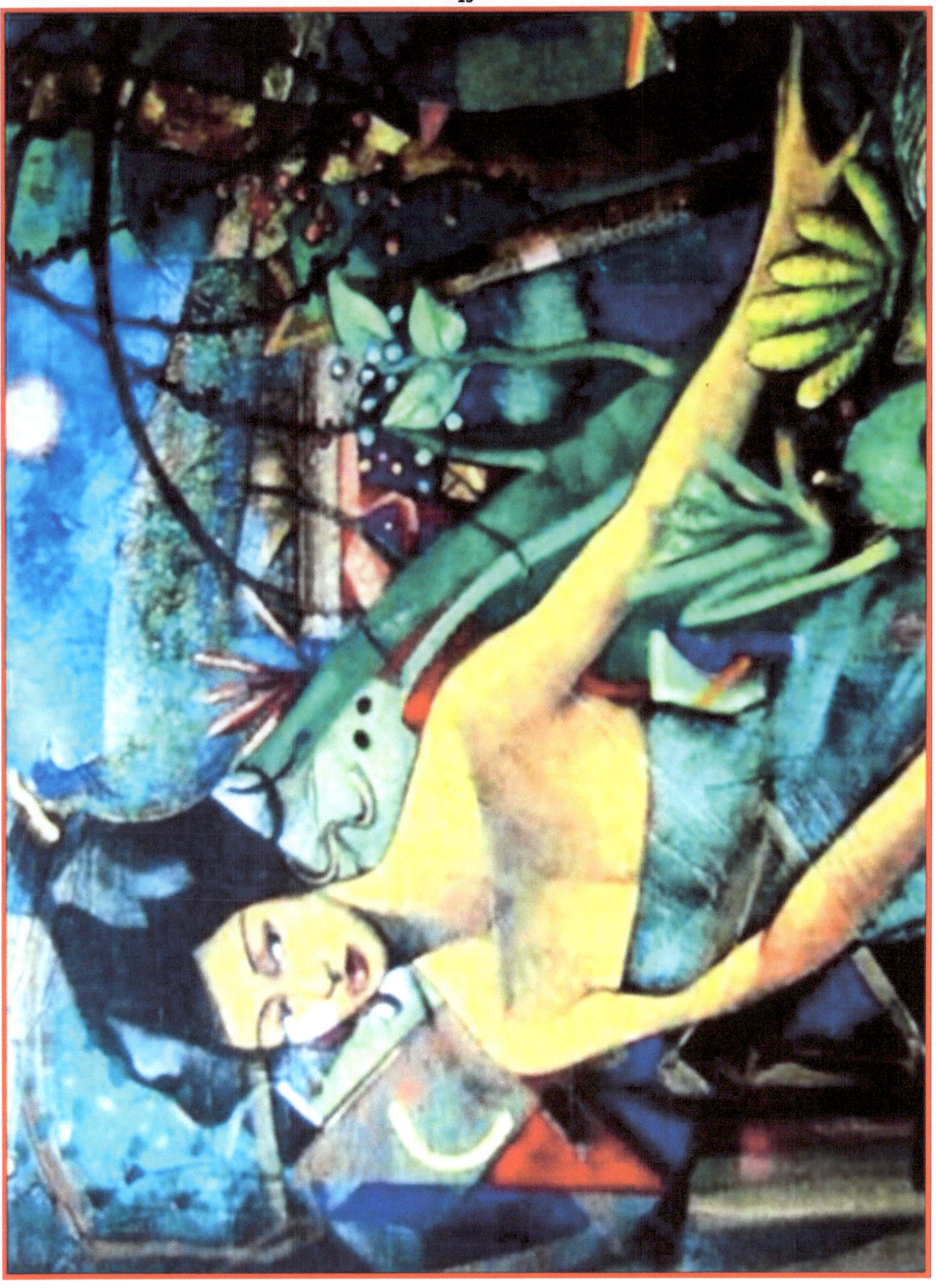

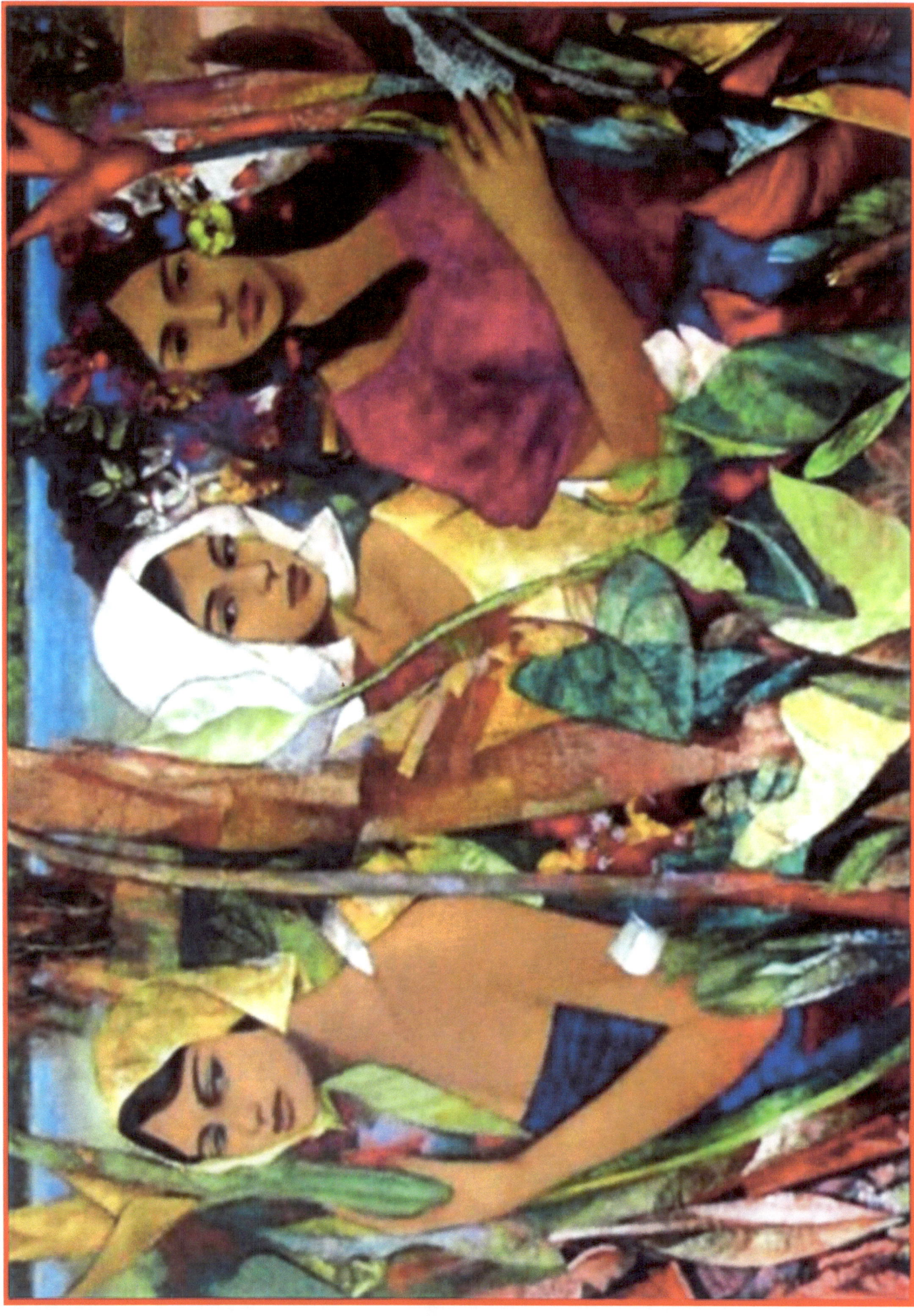

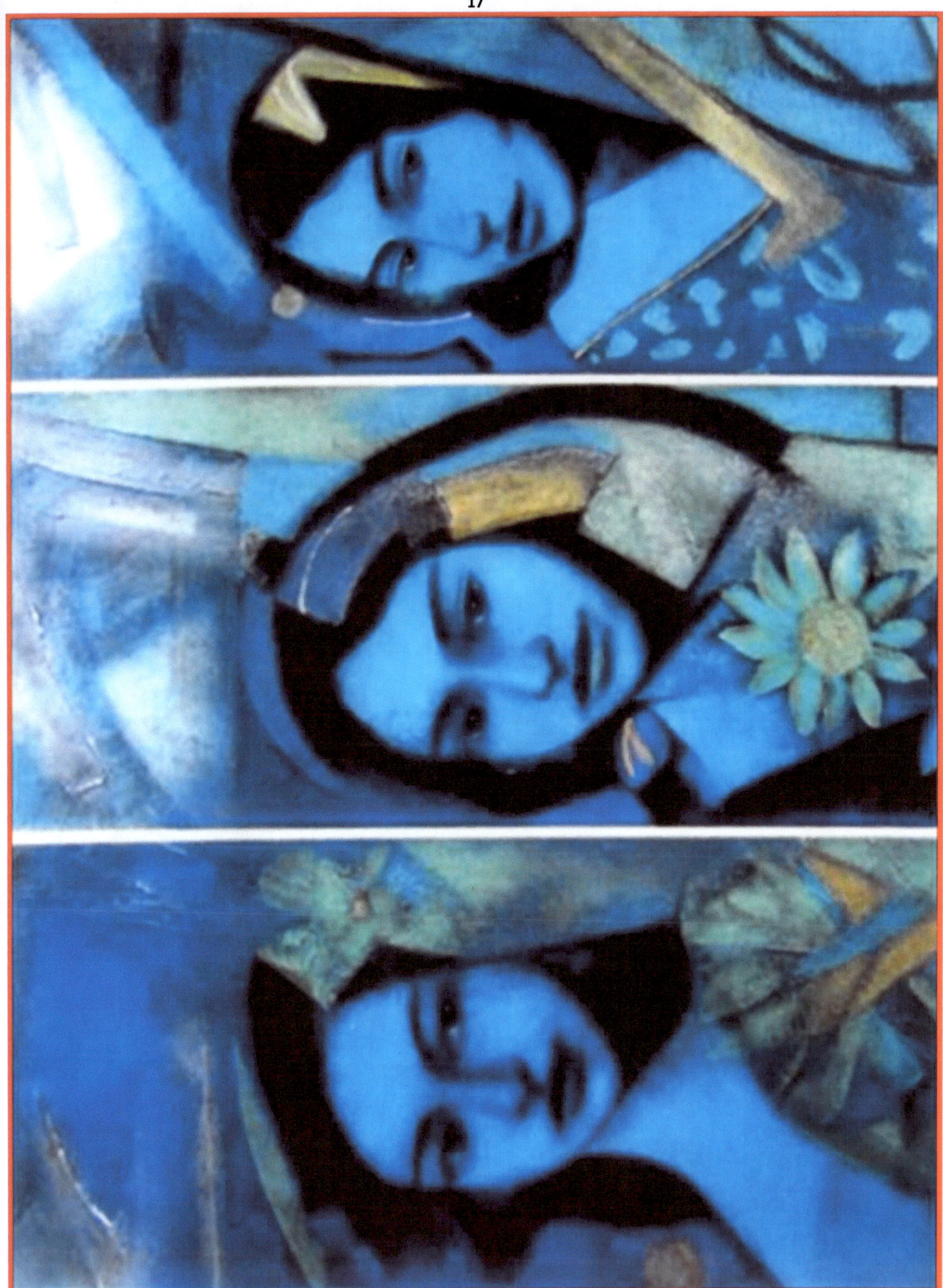

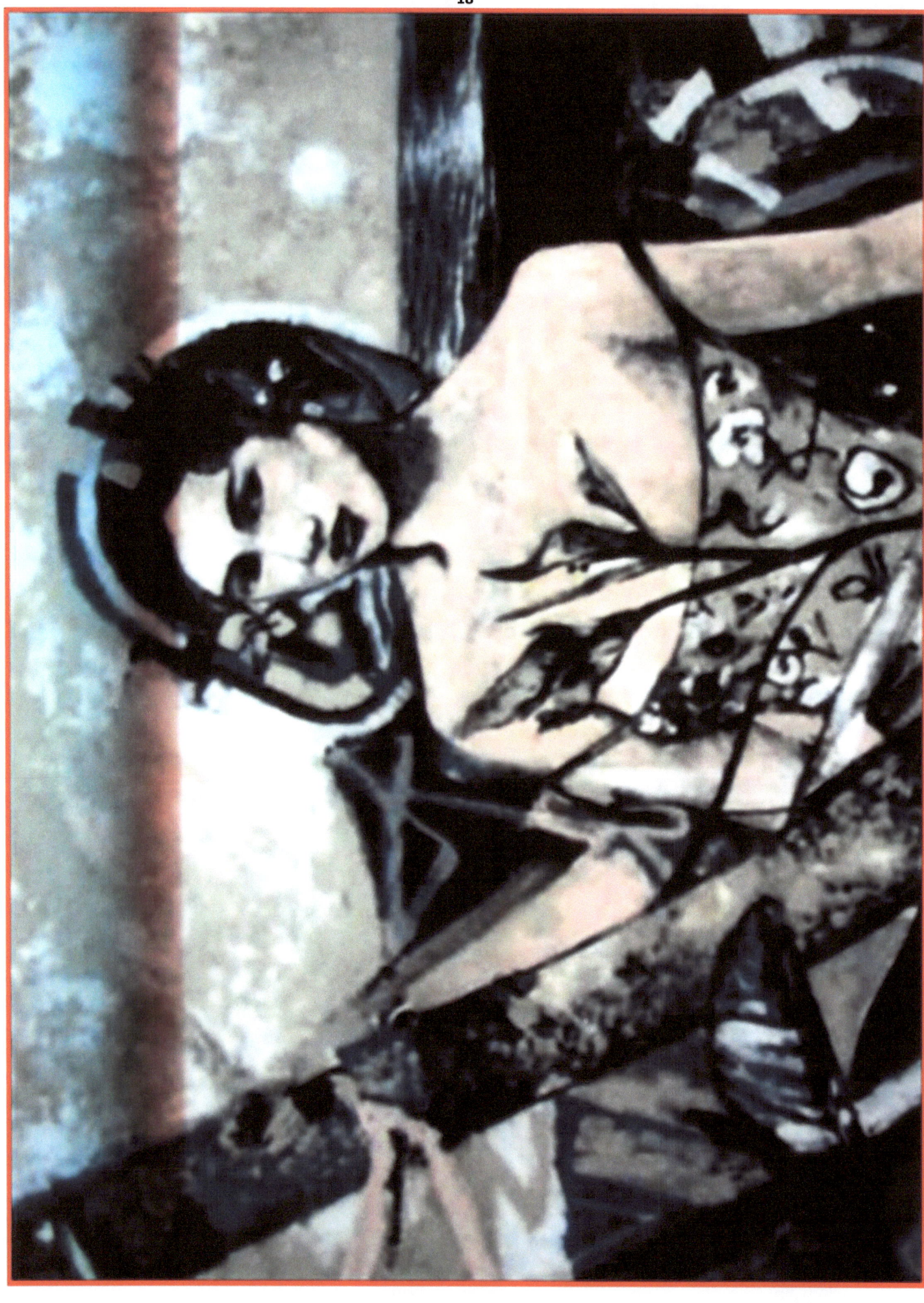

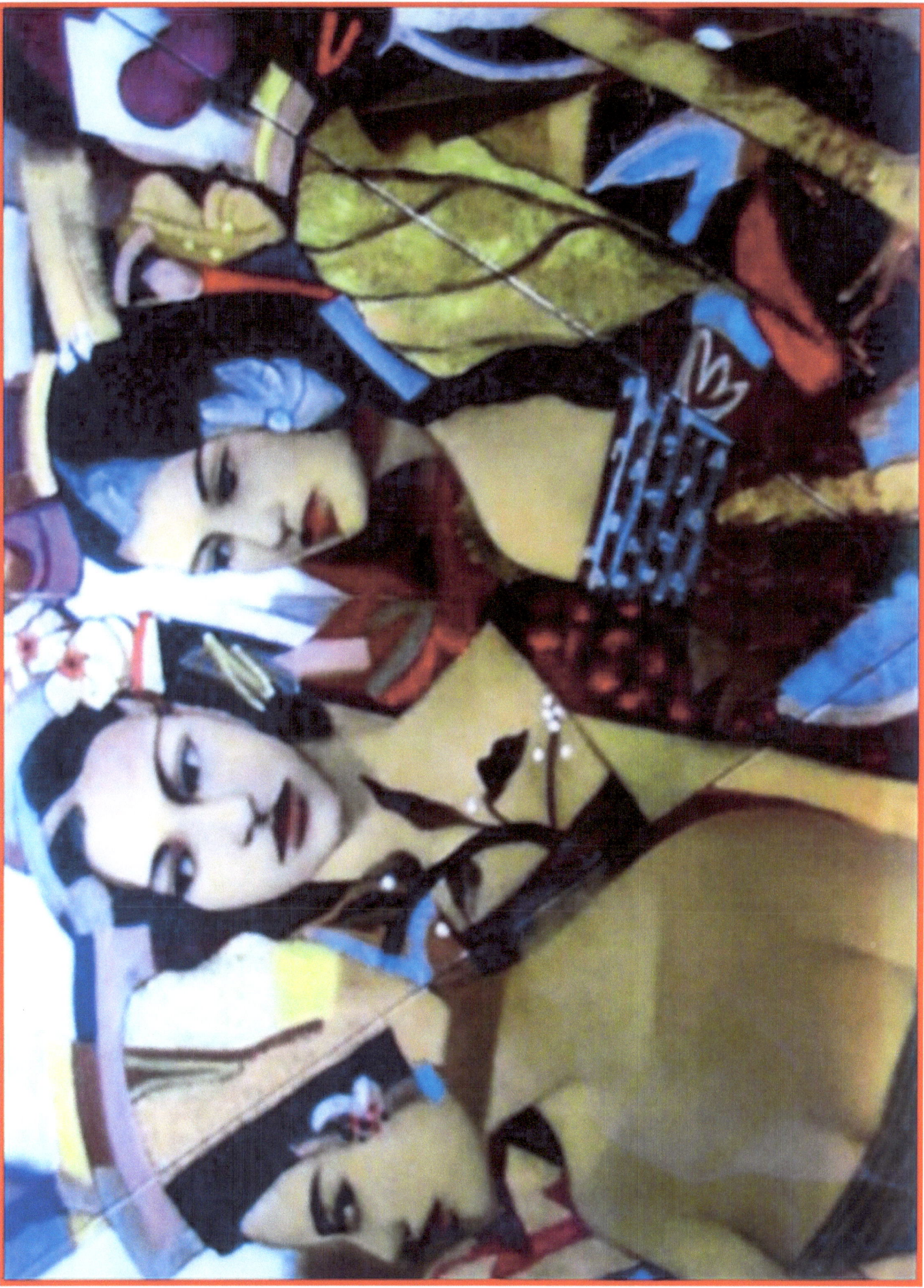

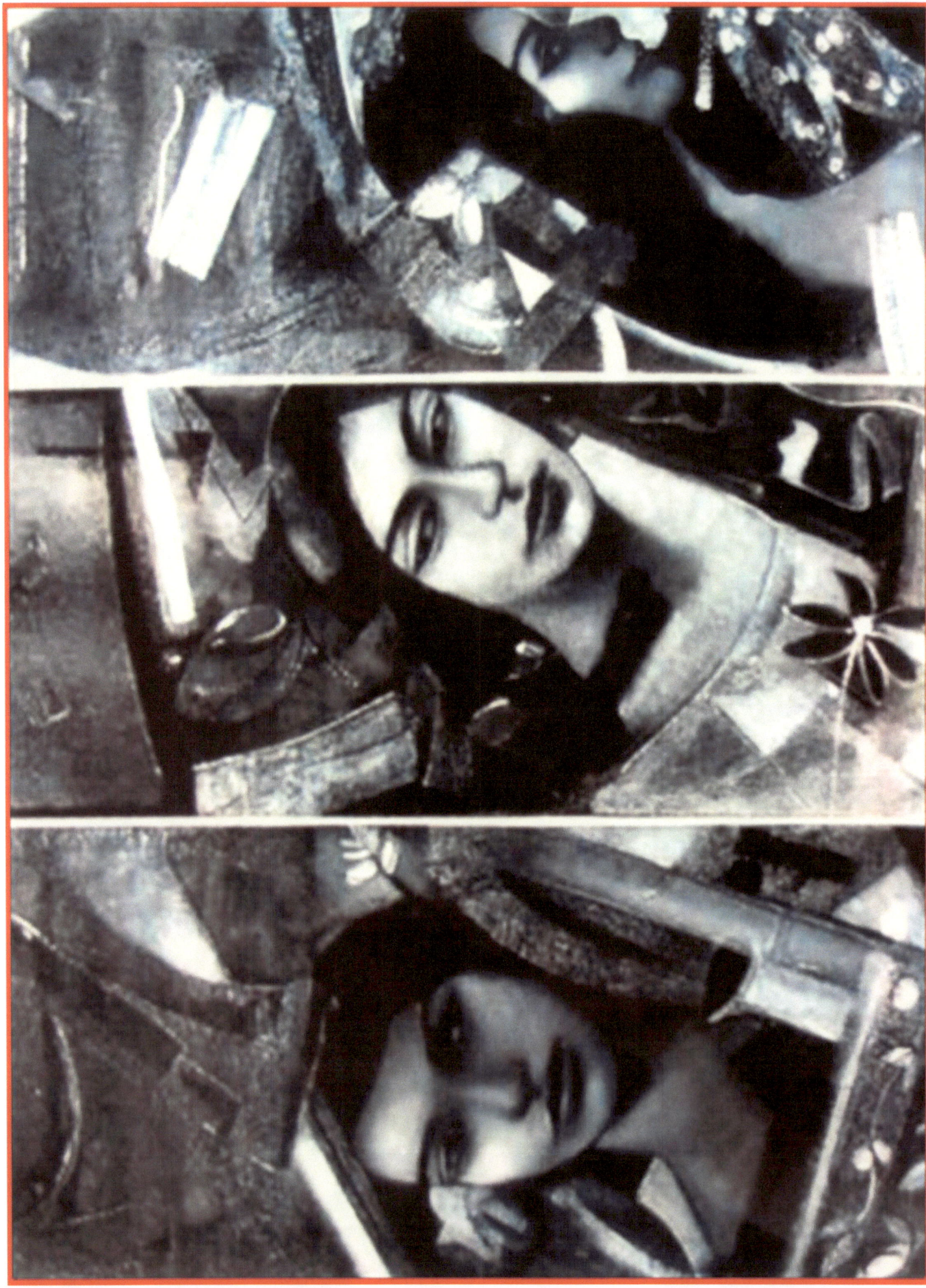

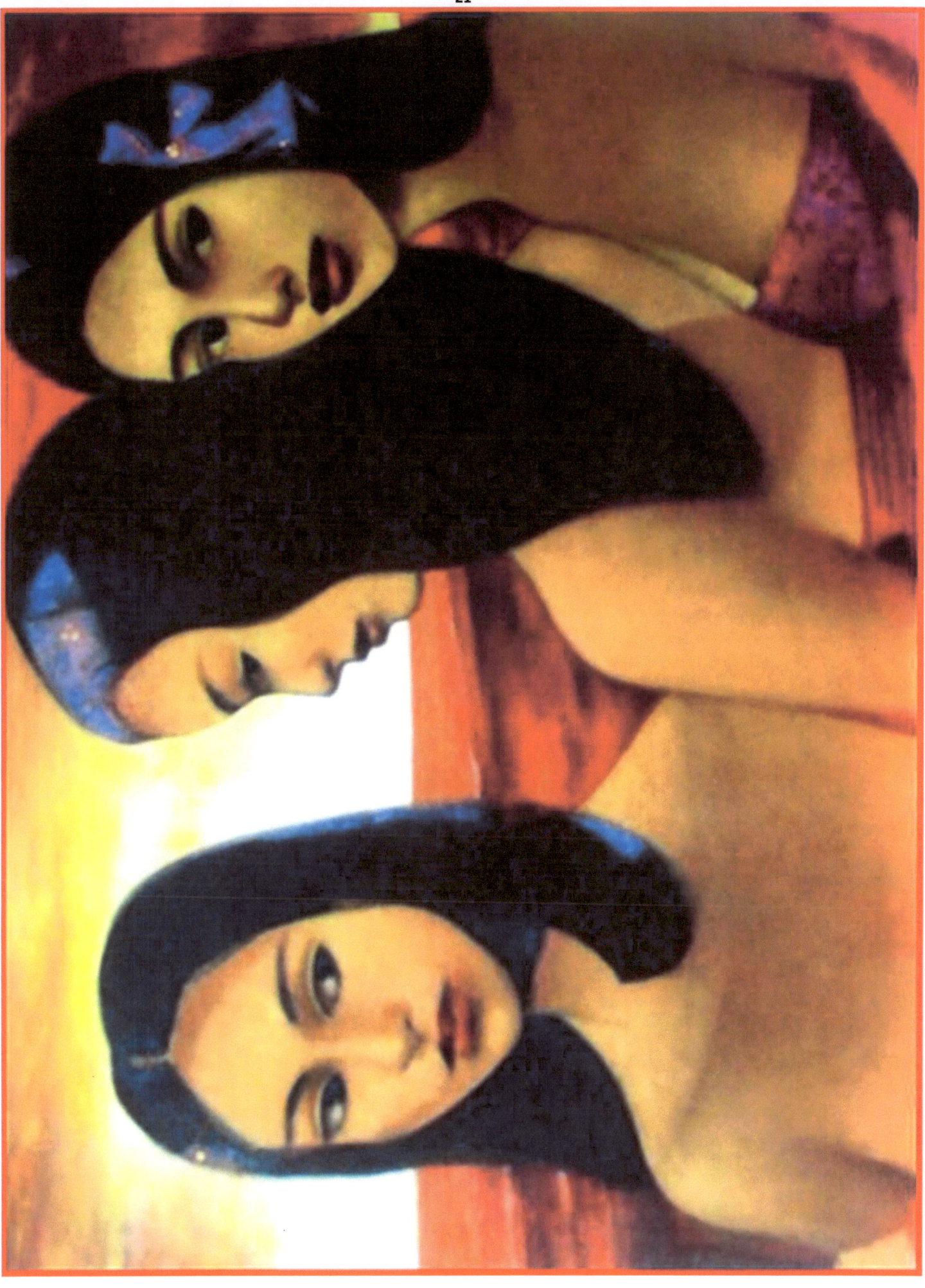

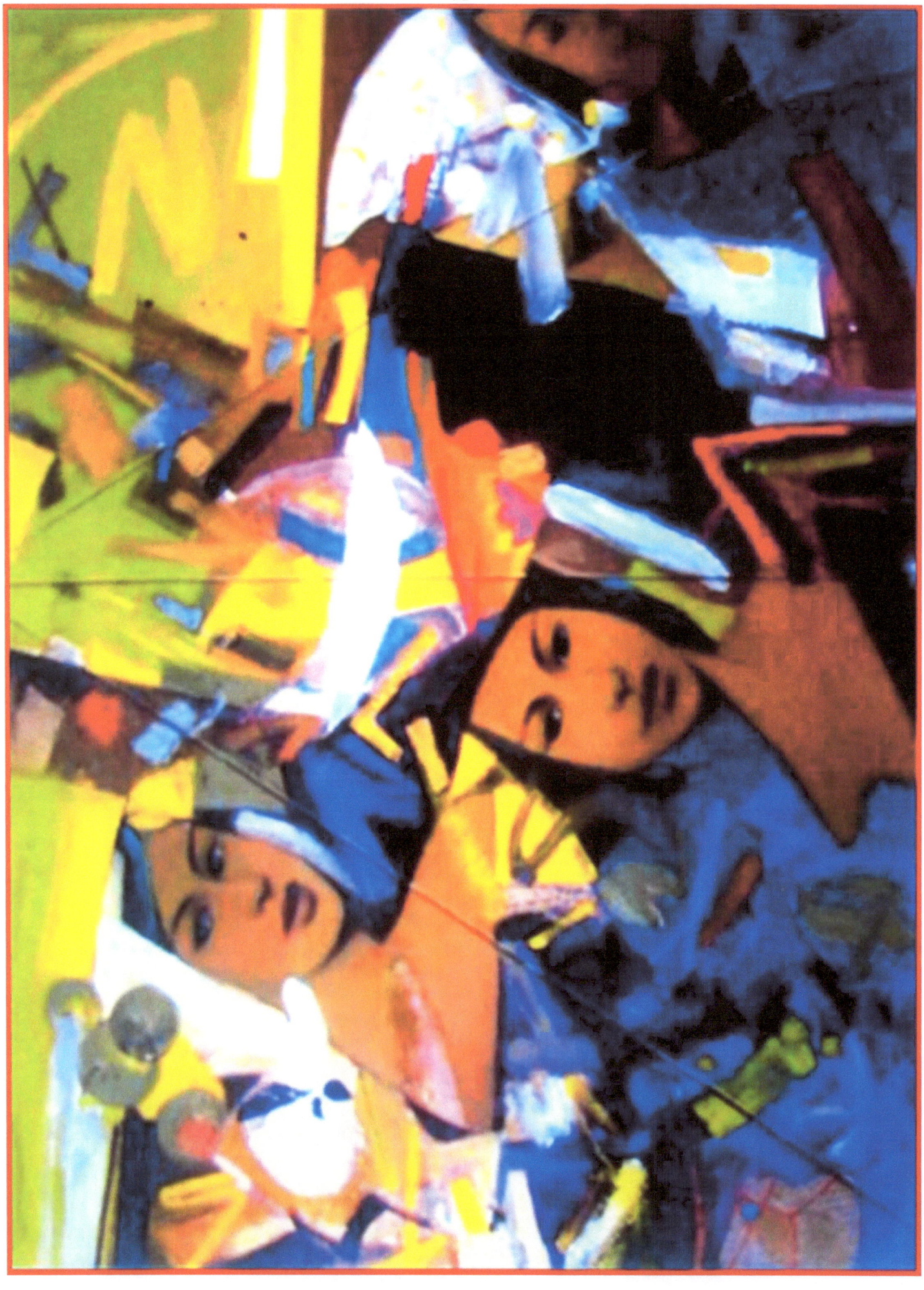

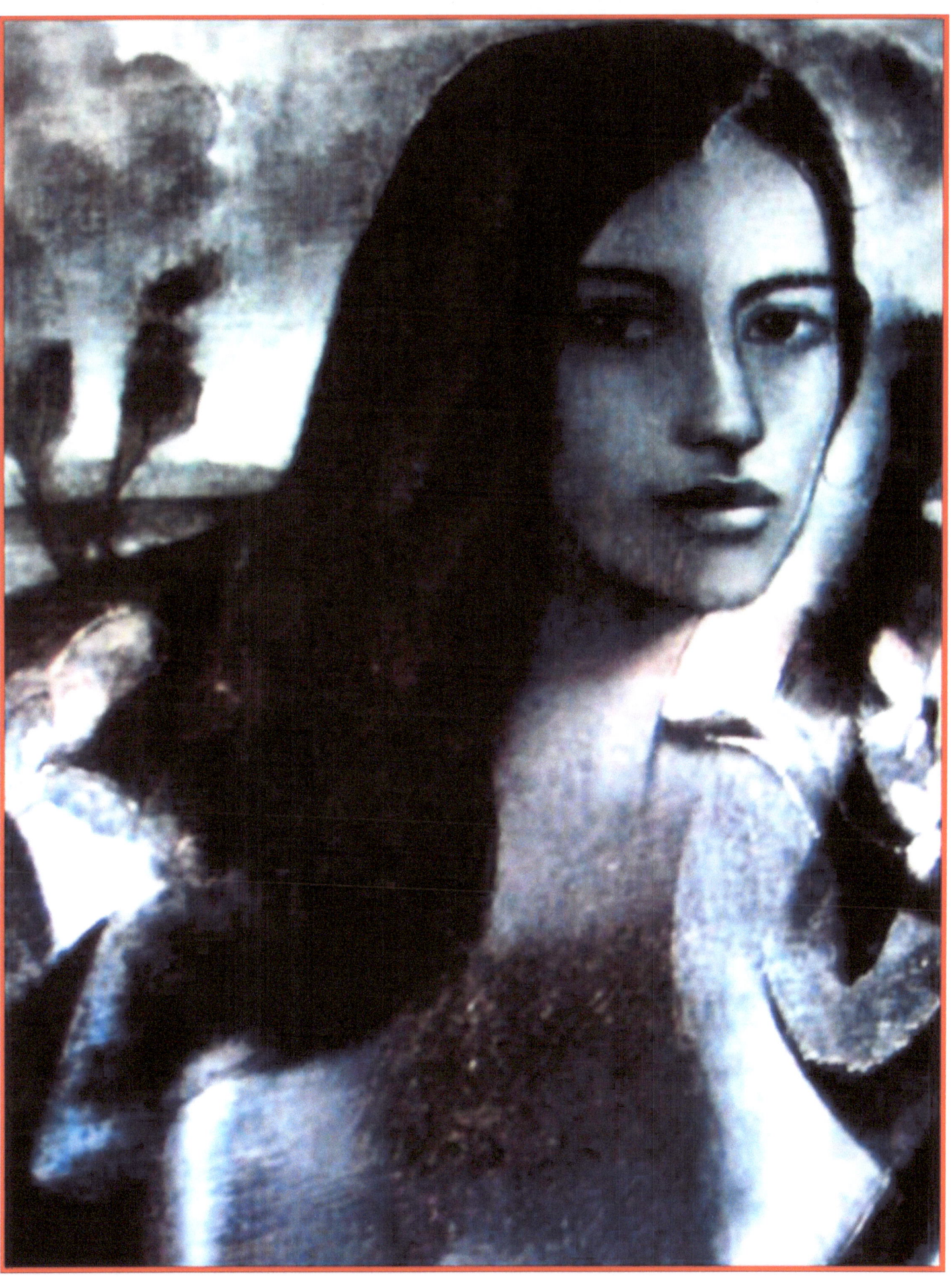

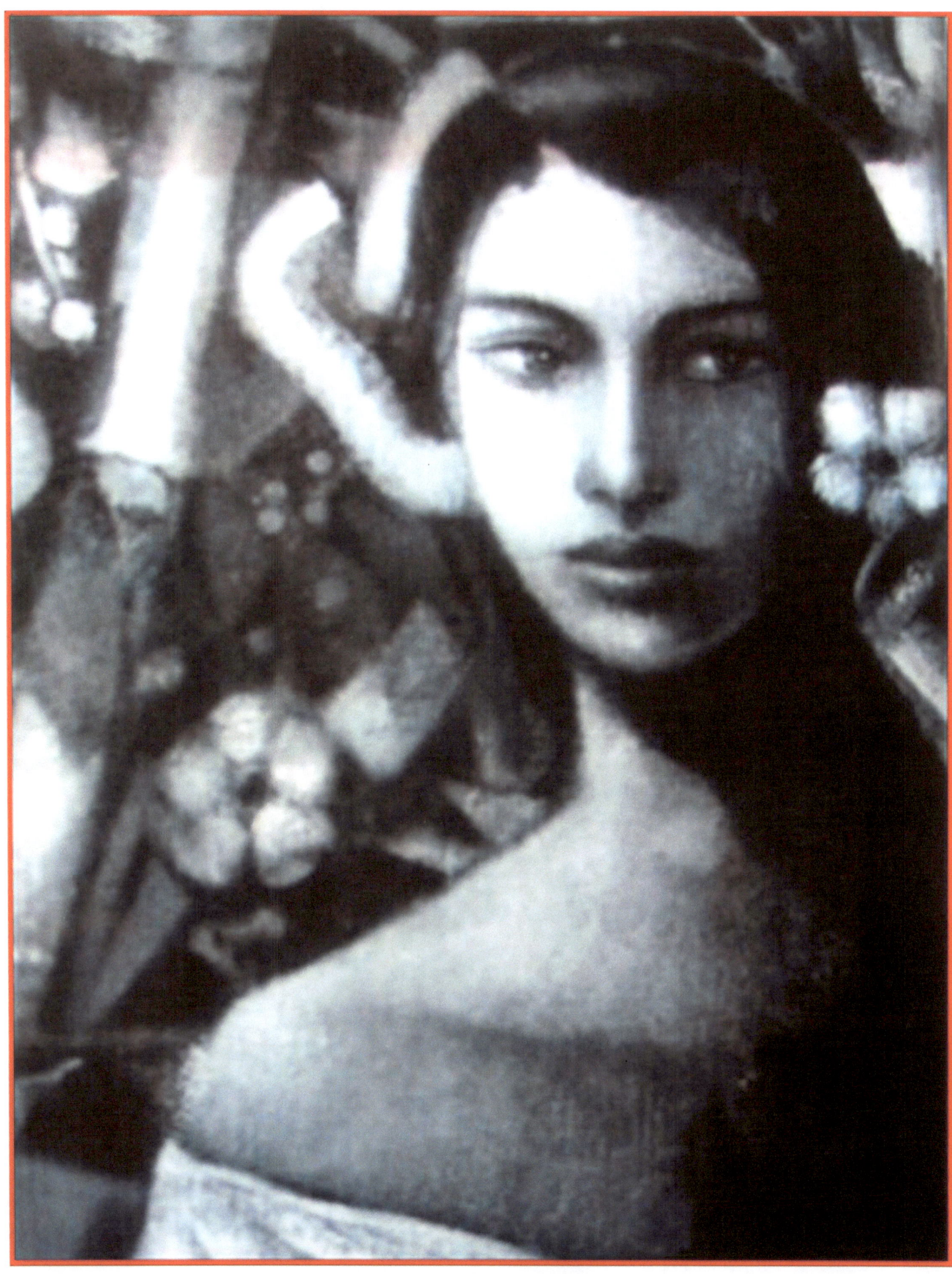

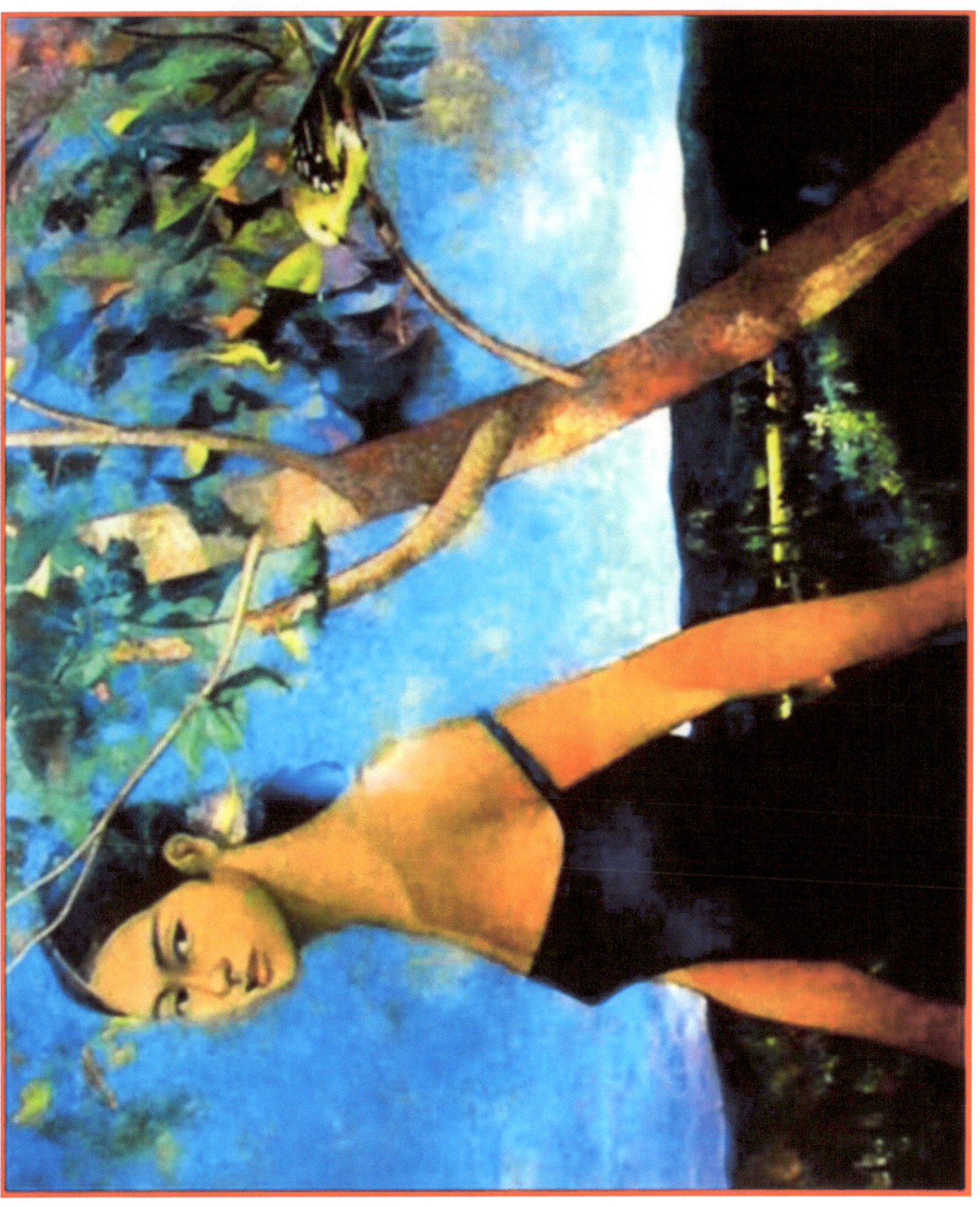

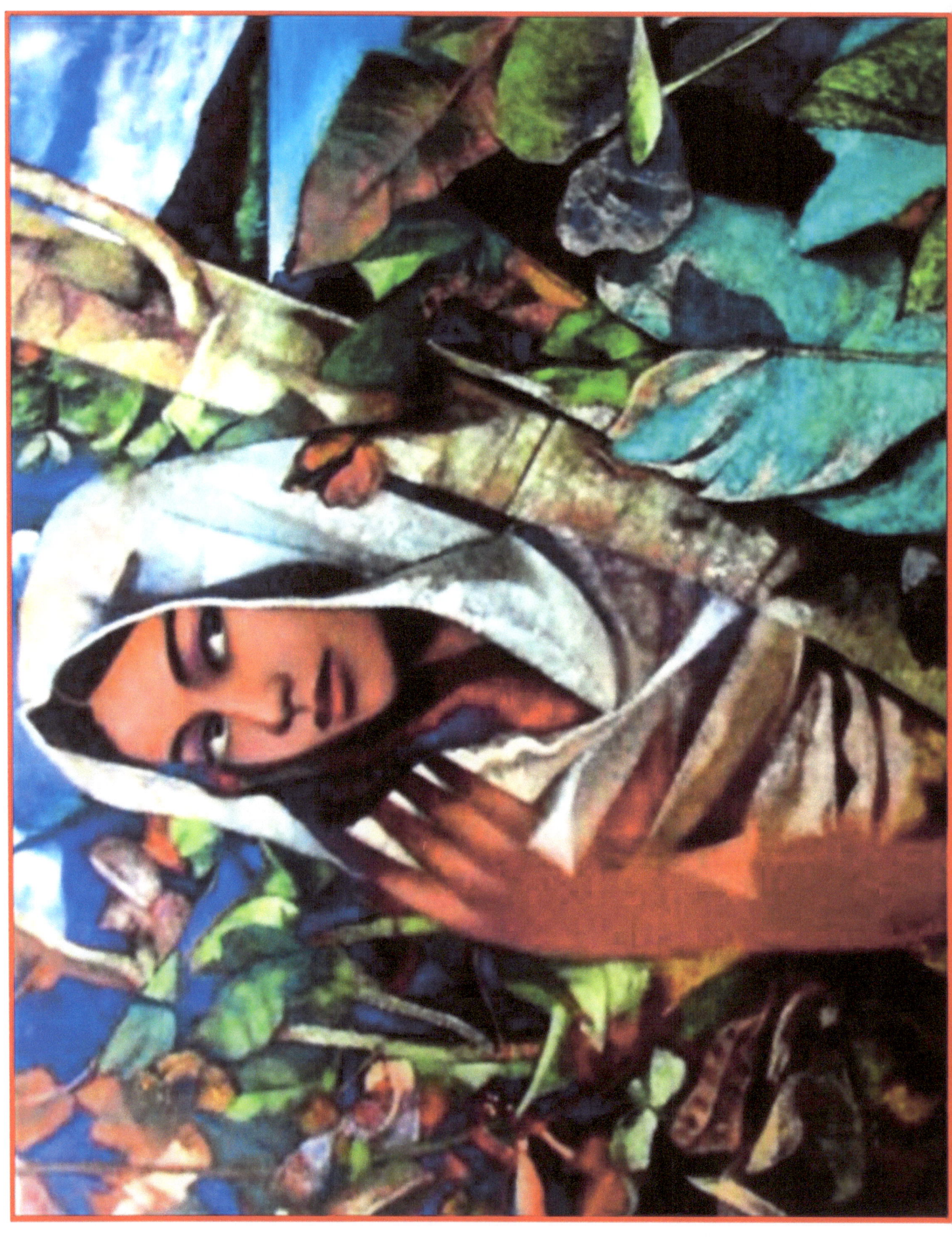

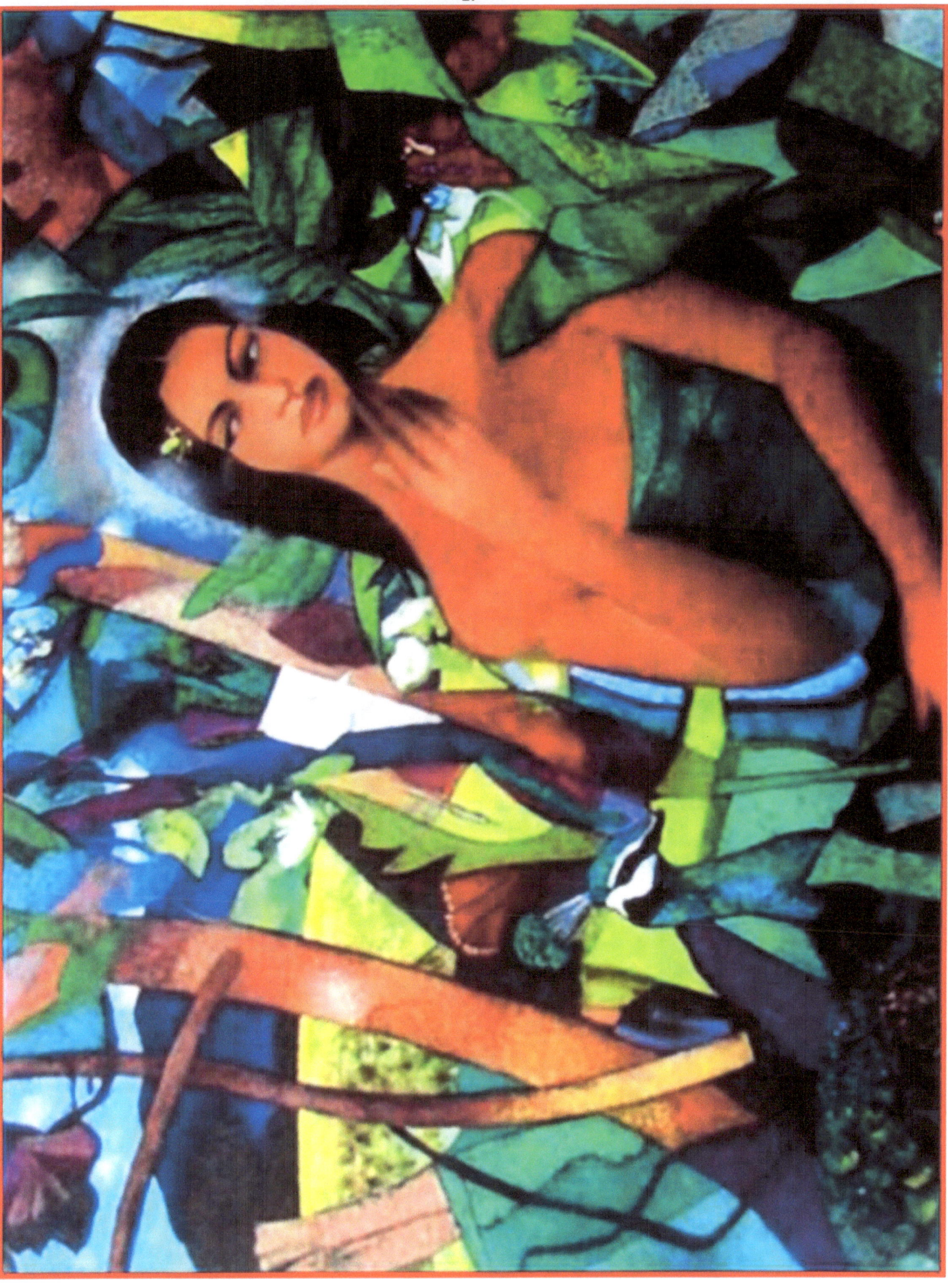

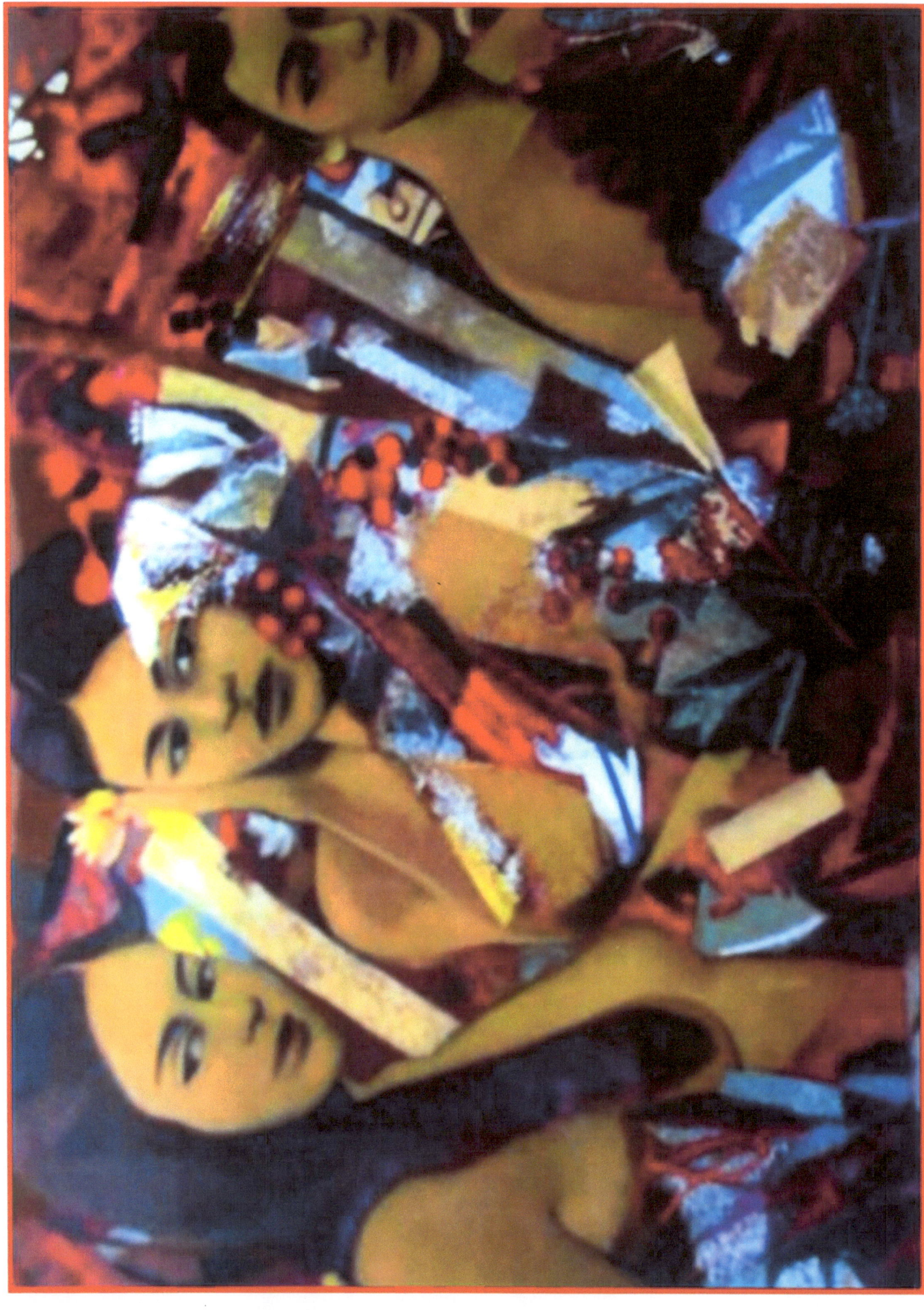

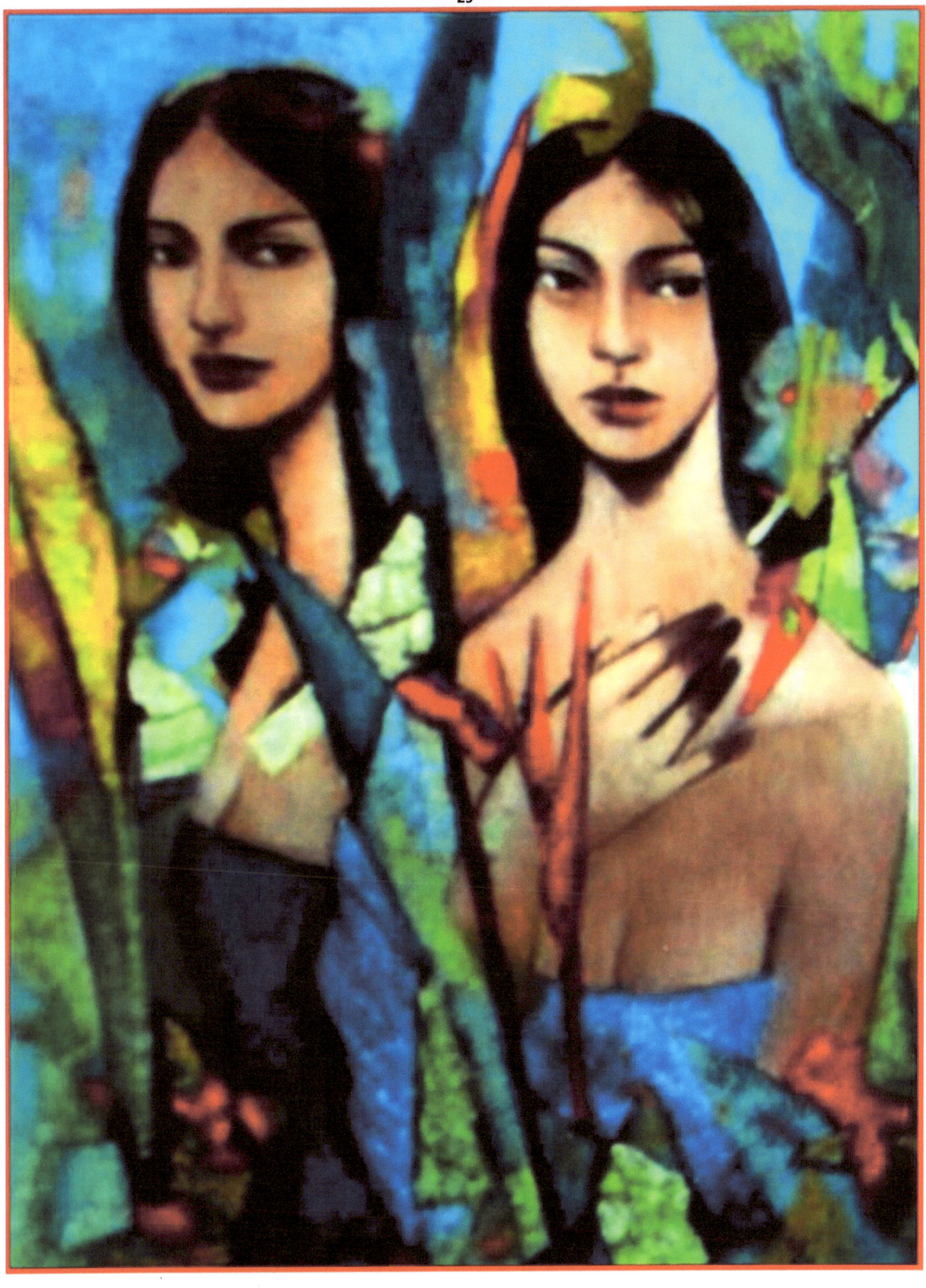

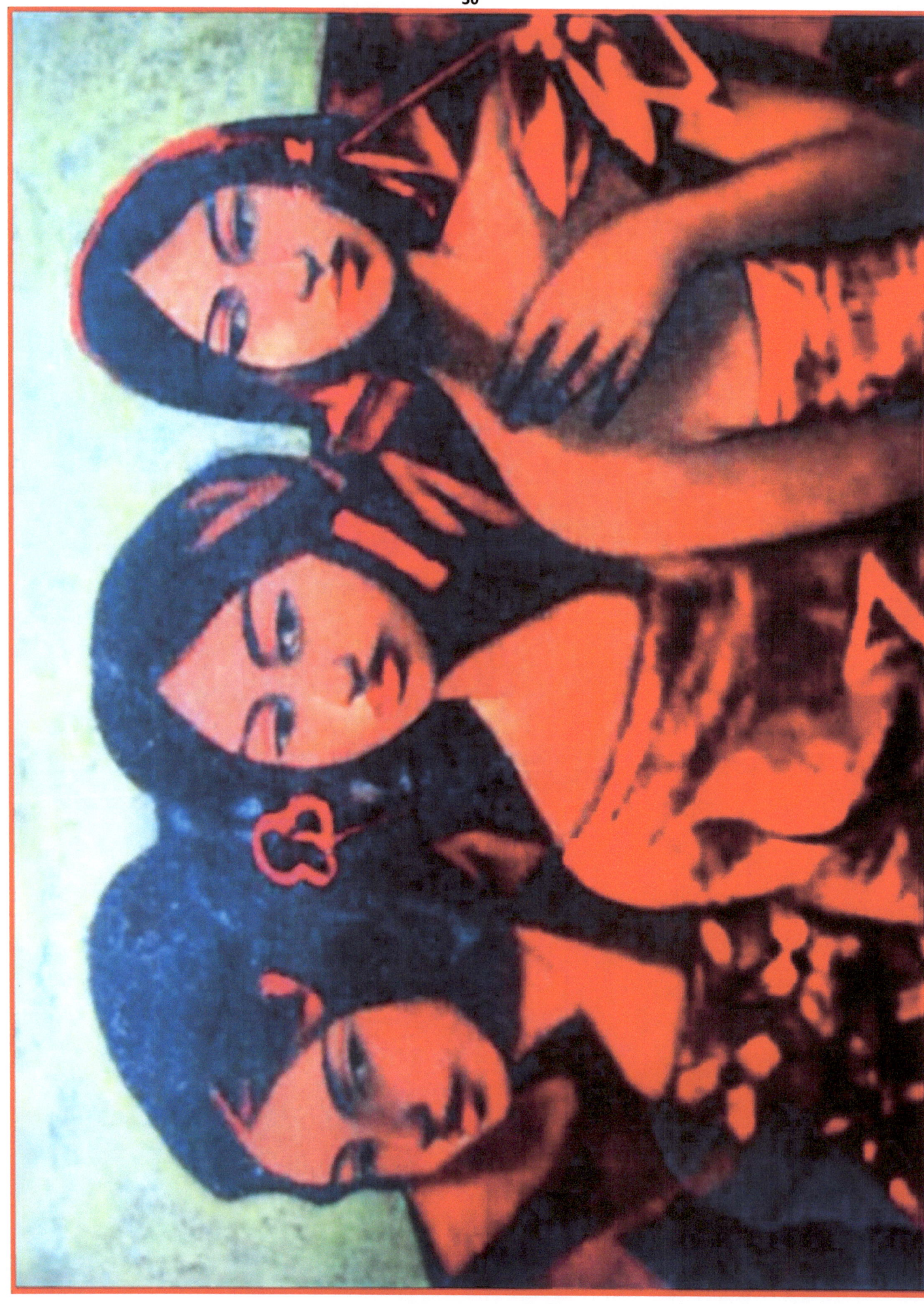

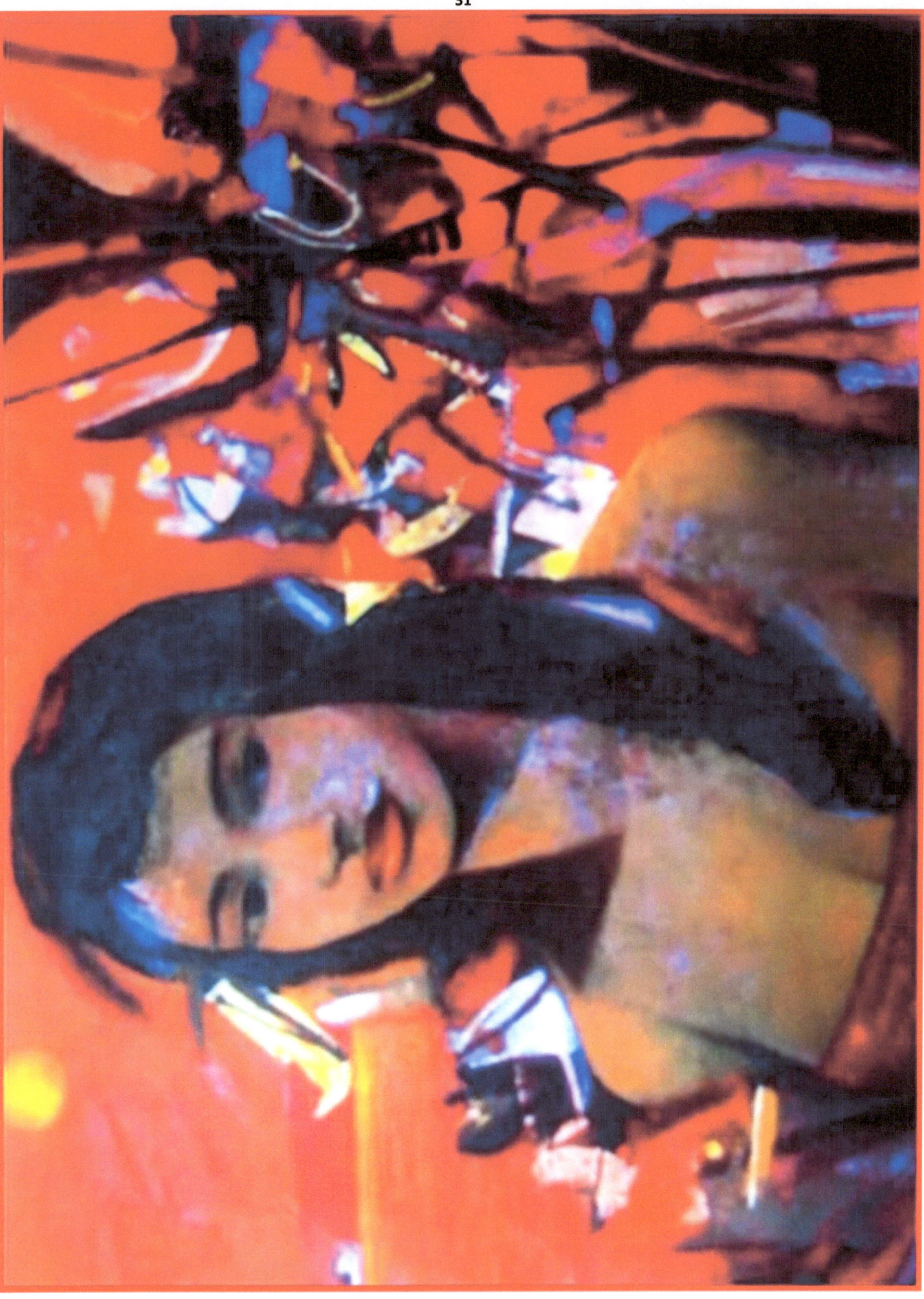

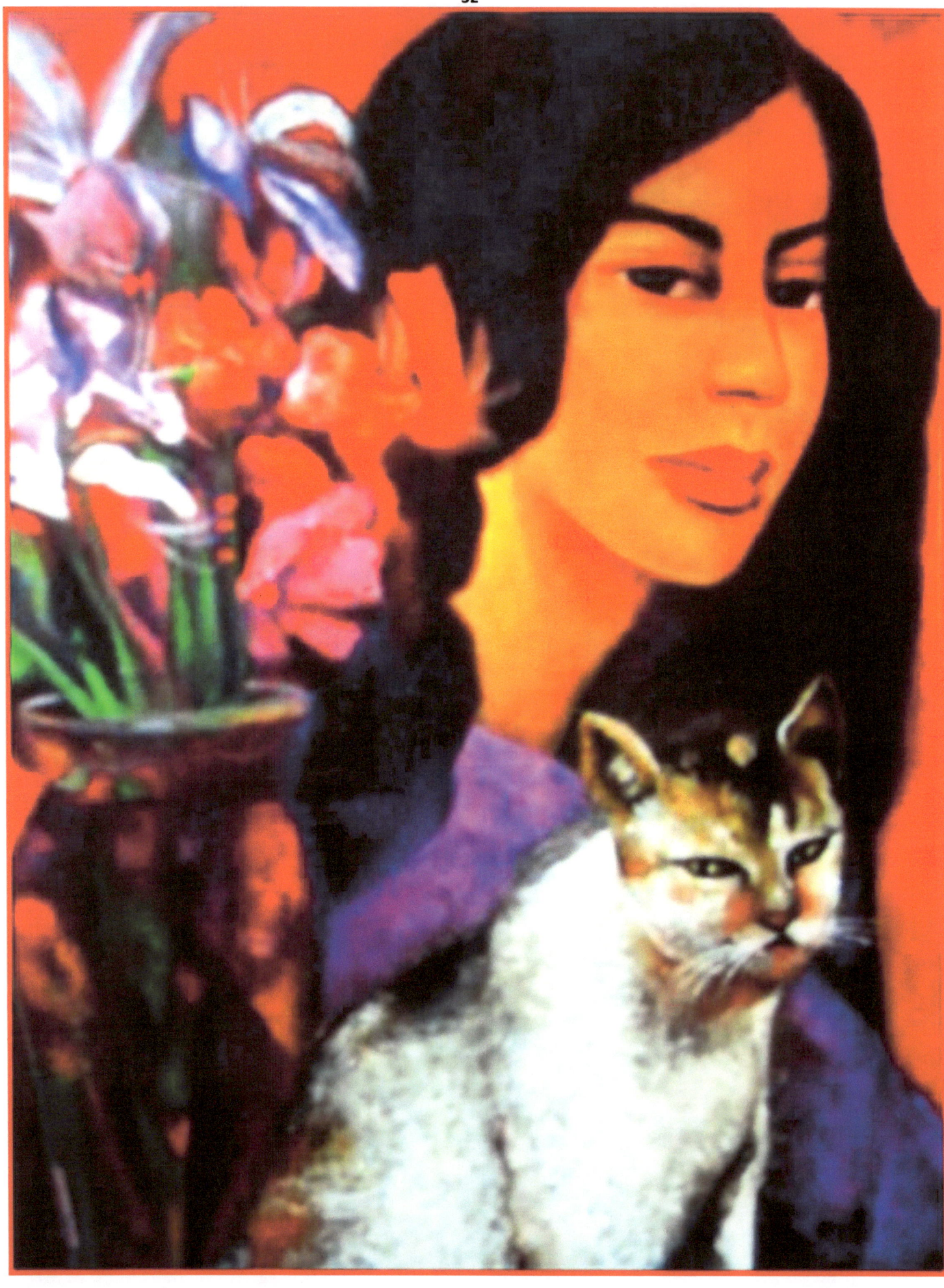

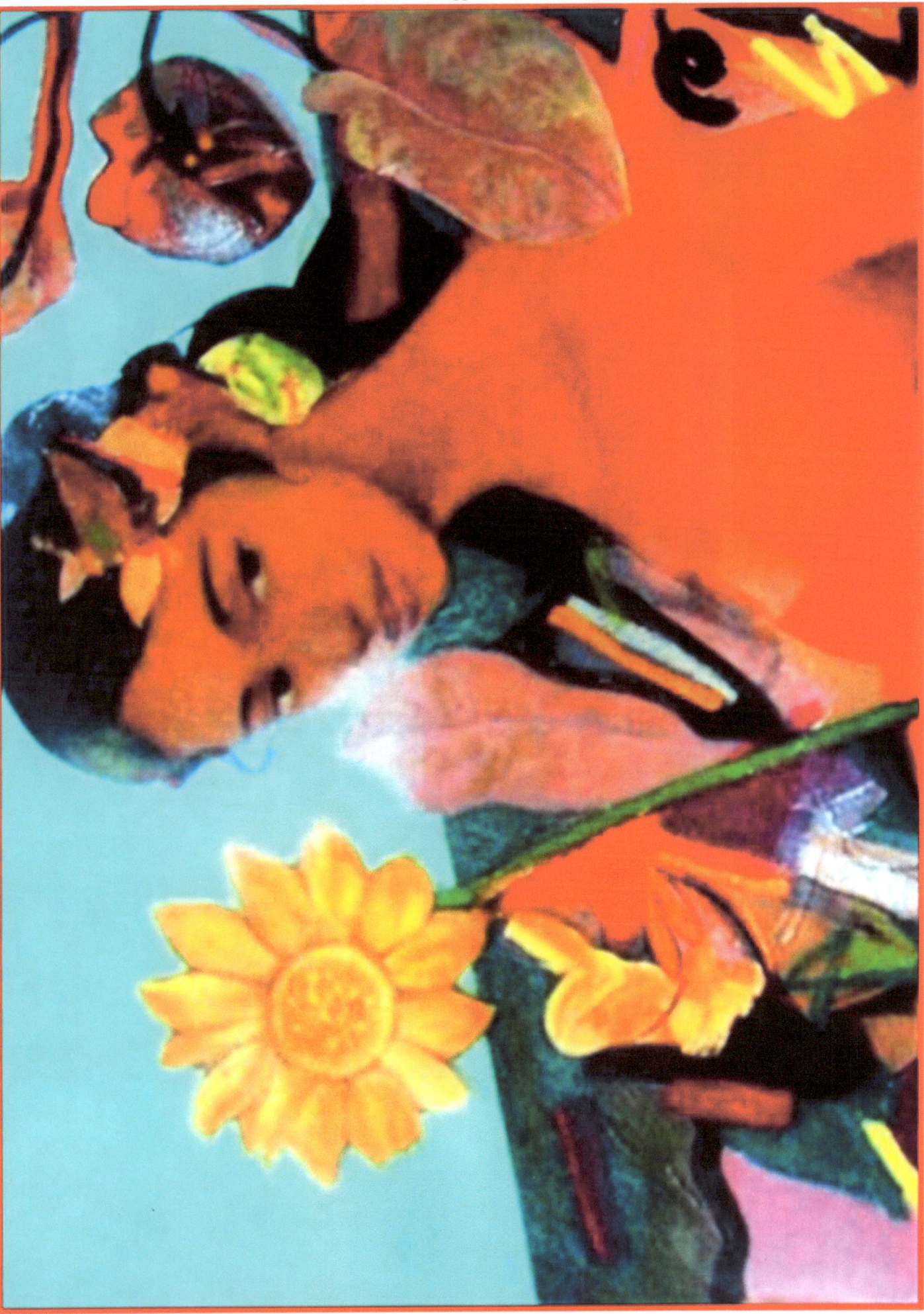

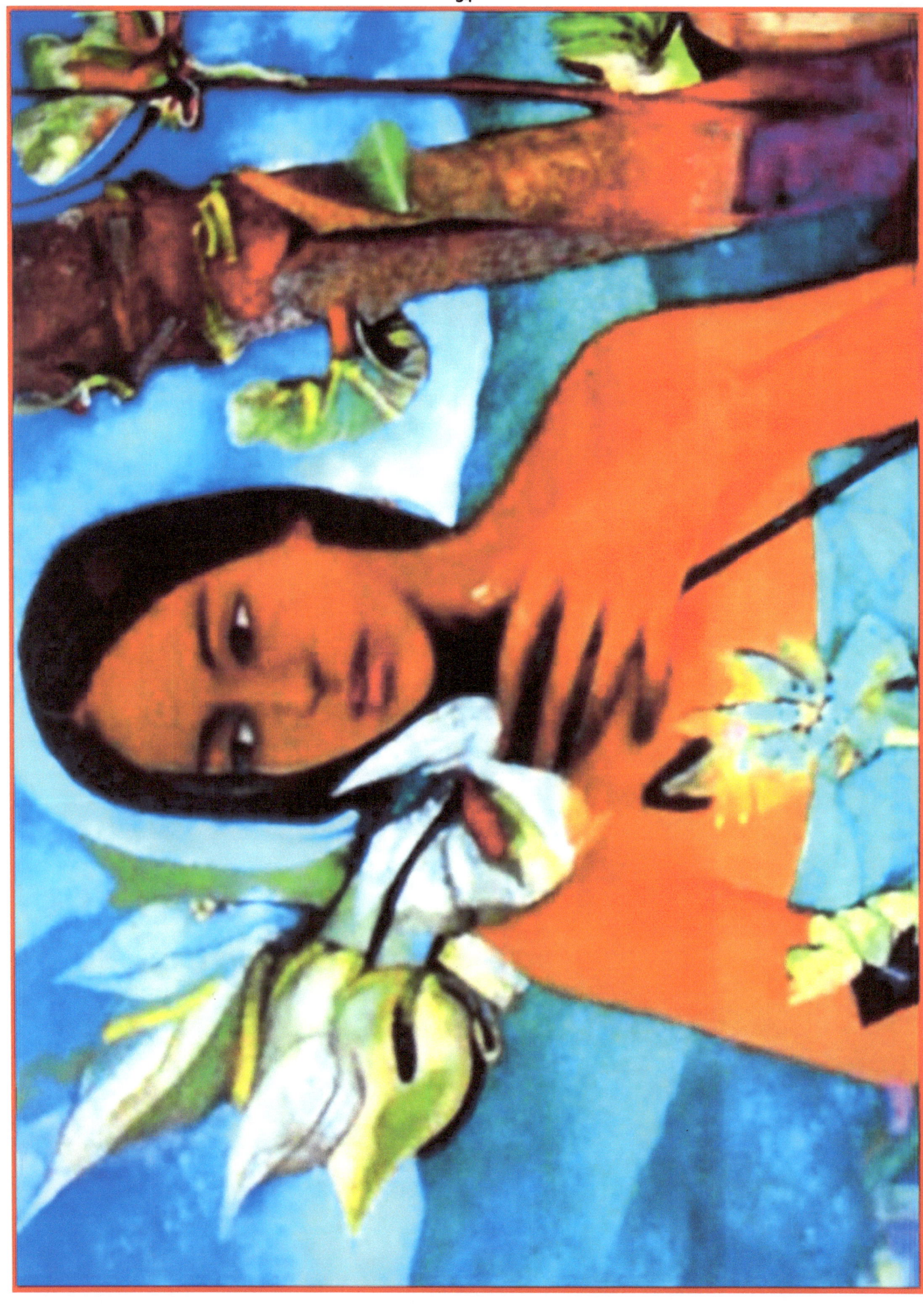

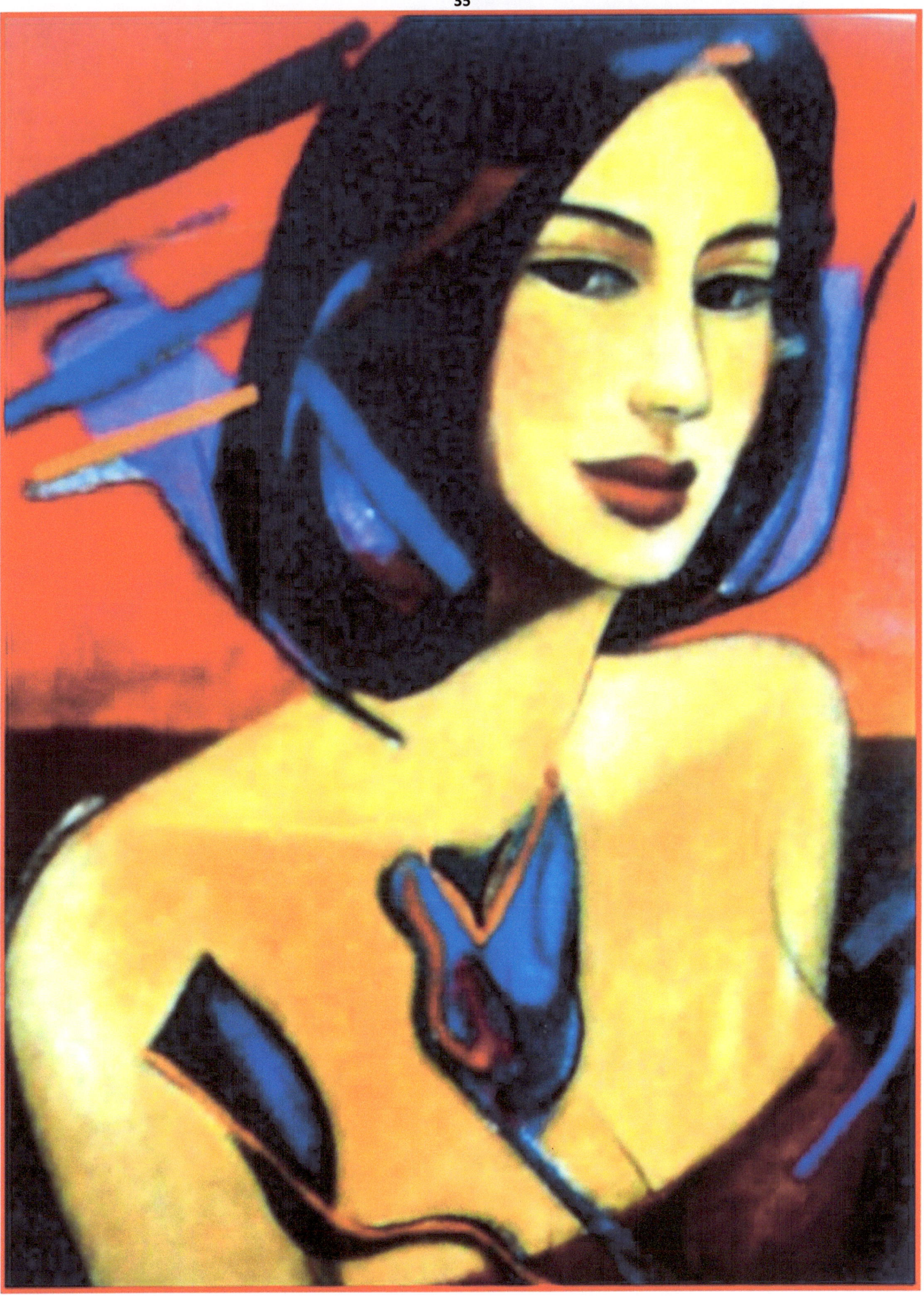

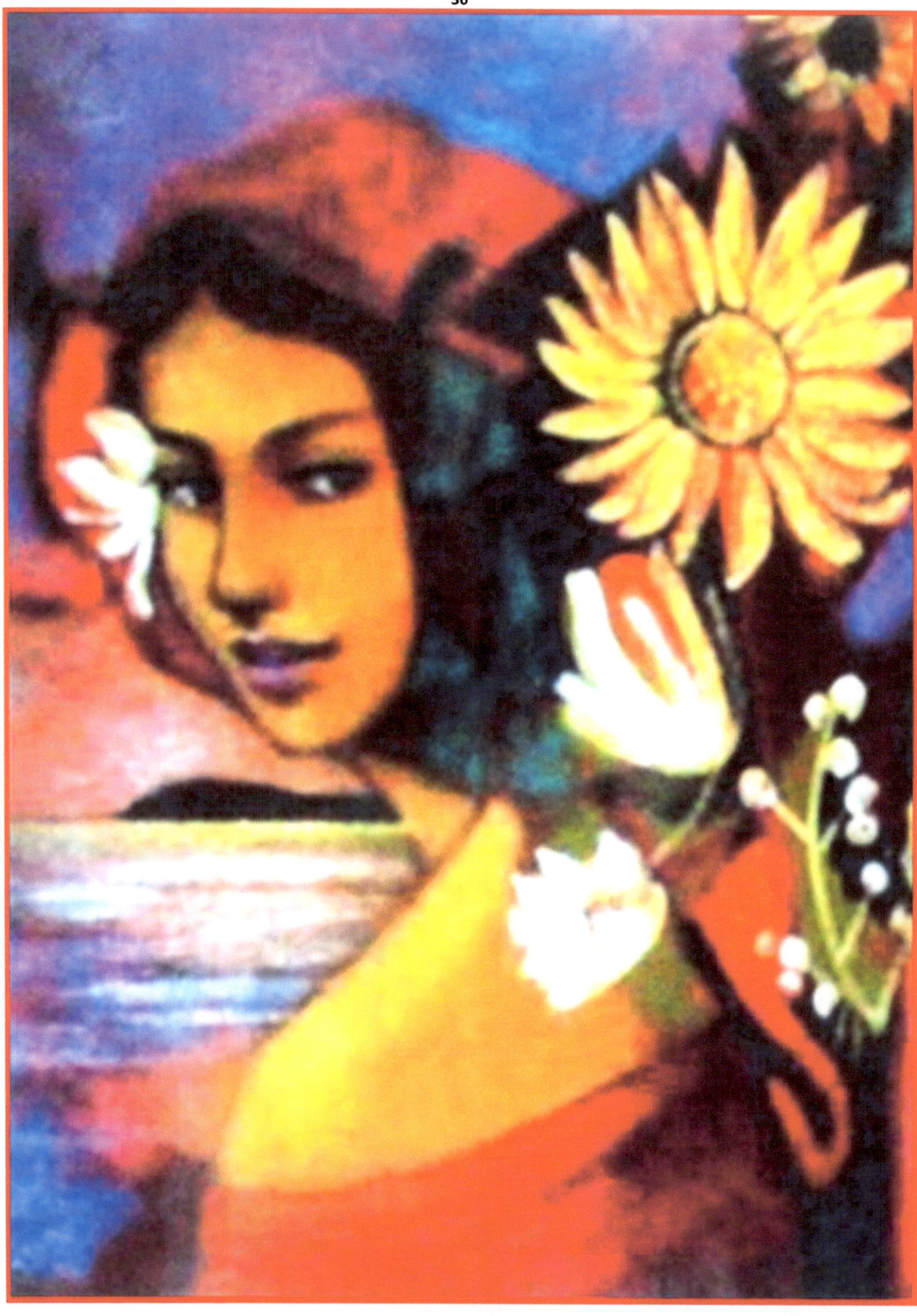

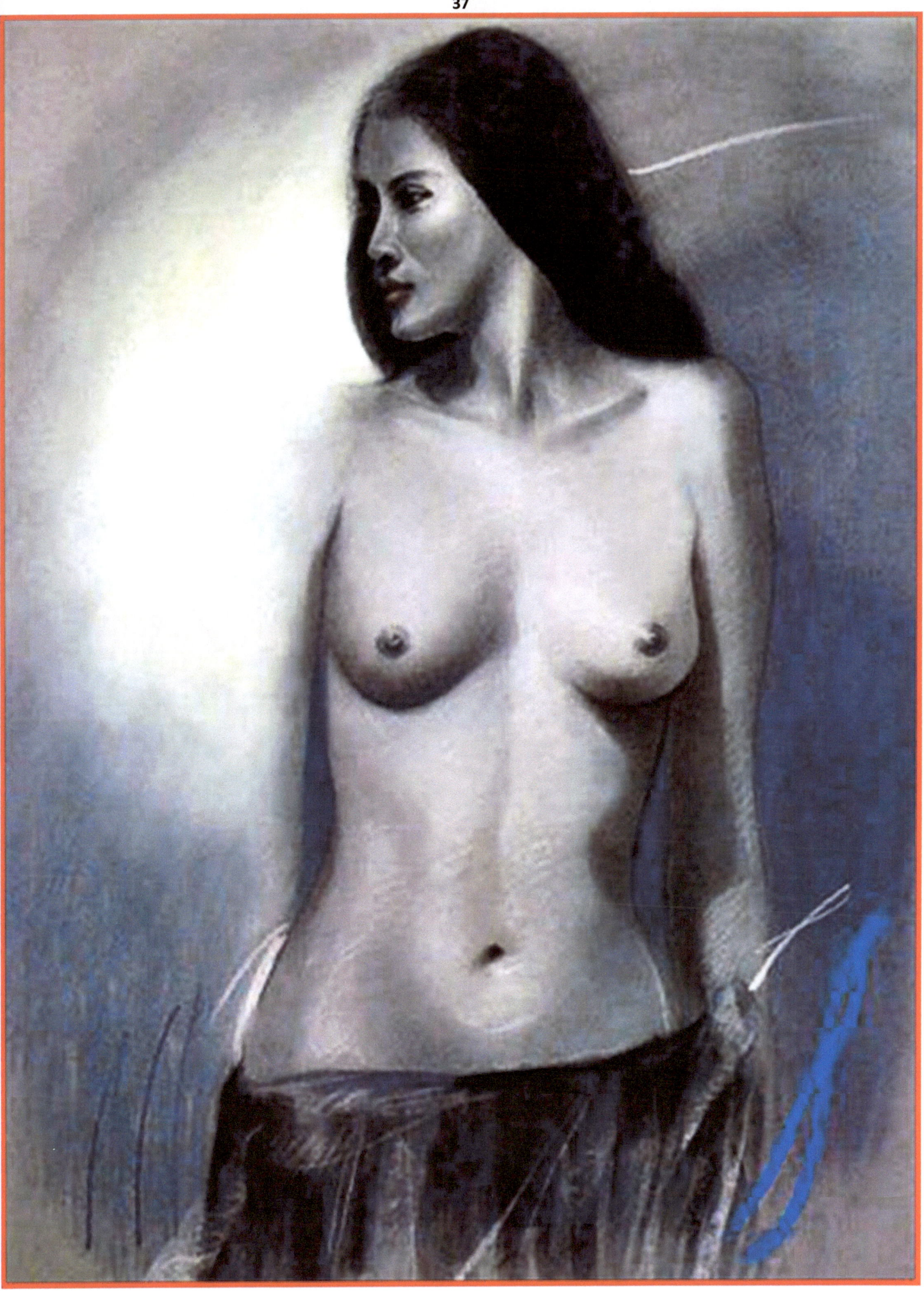

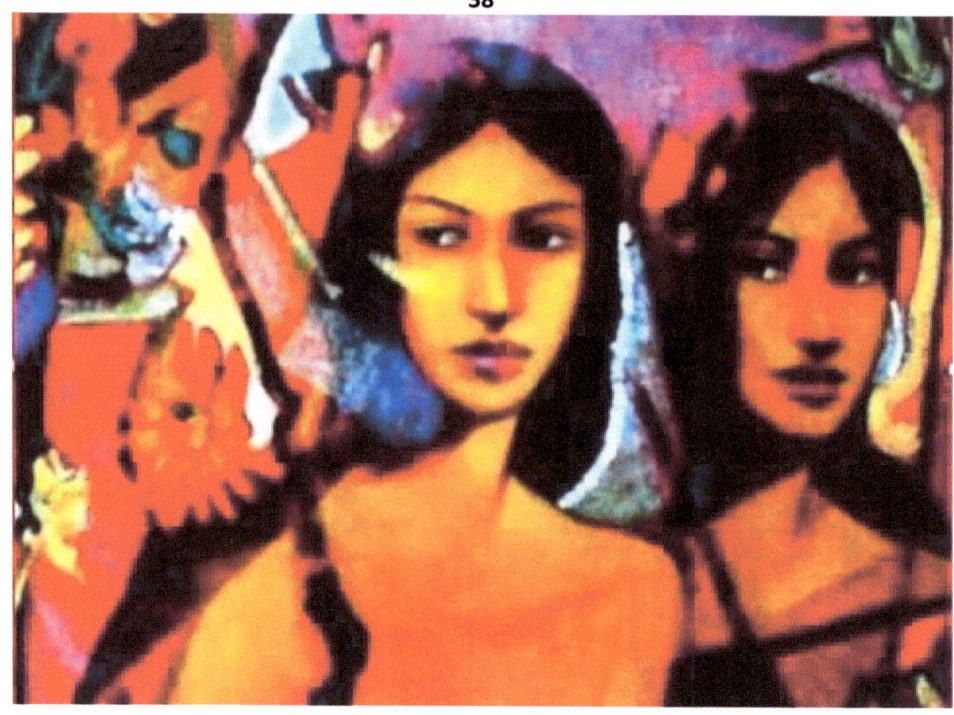

Tatay Jobo Elizes – Self-Publisher's Booklist

Writings 1 Book, 2009 + I. **Catch That Story** - *Tatay Jobo Elizes, publisher* + II. **Obit** - *Bambi Harper, Famous columnist* + III. **Speech, UP, 2003** - *Butch Jimenez, PLDT Executive* + IV. **Speech, Silliman U, 2006** - *Butch Jimenez, PLDT Executive* + V. **The Mission Moment** - *Dr. Phil Stack, Psyhologist* + VI. **Writing Underground** - *Mila D. Aguilar, Poet & Writer* + VII. **Academic Freedom** - *Mila Aguilar, Poet & Writer* + VIII. **Subanon Spirits of Rice & Land** - *Noel Cornel Alegre, Academician* + IX. **I Look Out The Window** - *Atty. Toto Causing, Lawyer, Journalist & Writer* + X. **Ride On A Bus, Poem** - *Anonymous via Melanie Ferrer, Budding Poet* + XI. **Why Am I Doing This** - *Susie Barbieri, Social Activist* + XII. **How To Court A Philipine Lady** - *Rodel Ramos & Jose Torres, Civic Leaders* + XIII. **Inspiring Young Filipino Entrepreneur** - *Lloyd Luna, Motivational Speaker* + XIV. **The Success Story of Ian Del Carmen** - *Lloyd Luna, Motivational Speaker* + XV. **Story of Bacna Surgical Mission** - *Sylvia Salvador, Civic Leader* + XVI. **1987 Philippine Constitution** - *Full Text (Special Feature)* + XVII. **Why Publish Writings** - *Tatay Jobo Elizes, Publisher*

Writings 2 Book, 2009 + I. **Why Can't We Act Up Together** - *Susie Barbieri, Social Activist* + II. **I Know Where They Are All Going** - *Cesar Lumba, Writer & Poet* + III. **There Is Hope For The Philippines** - *Grace Padaca, Isabela Governor* + IV. **Pointers On Employment Abroad** - *Melanie Aquino, Dentist & Writer* + V. **Without KNCHS: (Love story)** - *Atty. Toto Causing, Jury Proponent, Writer* + VI. **422 Years Ago** - *Rodel Rodis, Writer & Political activist* + VII. **Filipino American History Month** - *Rodel Rodis, Writer & Political activist* + VIII. **Love is the Next Truth, poem** - *Daniel Rodis, son of Rodel* + IX. **A Need For Reflection - Gloom** - *Cesar Torres, Politial Activist, academician* + X. **Our Purpose Driven Life** - *Joey Concepcion, RFM Pres. & GoNegosyo activist* + XI. **Did Ninoy Die For Nothing** - *Joey Concepcion, RFM Head & GoNegosyo Activist* + XII. **Why The Filipino Voted** - *Pablito Lim, Zambales Businessman* + XIII. **Life And Love, Poem** - *Nannette Yatco, Dentist, Fine Artist, Poet* + XIV. **Criteria - American Institute of Philanthropy** - *Charity Guidelines (Feature)* + XV. **Strangers In Our Own Country** - *Casiano Mayor Jr., Author & Writer* + XVI. **Coming Revolution In The Ballot** - *Cesar Lumba, Author & Writer* + XVII. **2009 - A Retrospective** - *Cesar Lumba, Author & Writer* + XVIII. **All Over The World** - *Vicente Rivera Jr., Short Story Writer* + XIX. **Harvest** - *Loreto Paras Sulit, Short Story Writer* + XX. **Things Your Burglar Won't Tell** - *Jude Tagaciudad, Writer* + XXI. **The Gypsy Soul** - *Casiano Mayor Jr., Author & Writer* + XXII. **An End To Cheating** - *Sonny Coloma, Academician & Writer* + XXIII. **Toward Culture of Giving** - *Sonny Coloma, Academician & Writer*

Writings 3A Book, 2012 + + 1. **EPIC25, Emerging Philippines Investors Coalition**, *Norman Madrid* + + 2. **Management Ability As An Issue**, *Dr. Rene B. Azurin* + + 3. **Do We Really Want To Give Our Politicos More Power**, *Dr. Rene B. Azurin* + + 4. **Will 2010 Fulfill Filipinos High Hopes For Better Life – Metamorphosis**, *Ernie D. Delfin* + + 5. **Comelec Is The Root Of All Evils**, *Toto Causing* + + 6. **Some Advantages of Federalism and Parliamentary Government For The Philippines**, *Dr. Jose Abueva* + + 7. **Sometimes A Great Nation**, *Mar-Vic Cagurangan* + + 8. **Great Conspiracy**, *Mar-Vic Cagurangan* + + 9. **Of Speech & Life's Riddles**, *Casiano Mayor* + + 10. **Bad Start To The Year**, *Rod Garcia* + + 11. **A Dinner out**, *Rod Garcia* + + 12. **One More Time**, *Roy Gaane* + + 13. **Strange Noises** – *Tatay Jobo Elizes* + +

Writings 3B Book, 2012 + + 1. **The Reeds and Beams of Sunset in Paite and Balangaging in Zambales**, *Ceres Busa* + + 2. **Memories of your Past**, *Ceres Busa* + + 3. **Blowout in the Barrio**, *Ceres Busa* + + 4. **Dream on Sari-sari Store Keeper**, *Ceres Busa* + + 5. **O Naraniag O Bulan**, *Ceres Busa,* + + 6. **Candelaria, O Candelaria**, *Ceres Busa* + + 7. **Four P's … Pastillas, Pilipig, Patupat at Panan**, *Ceres Busa* + + 8. **On Being Filipino American**, *John Reyes* + + 9. **The Monterey Peninsula**, *John Reyes* + + 10. **The Salaza Fiesta**, *John Reyes* + + 11. **Salawikain: Filipino Proverbs**, *John Reyes* + + 12. **Musikero (The Musician)**, *John Reyes* + + 13. **Did You Know (1)**, *Bert Guiang* + + 14. **Did You Know (2)**, *Bert Guiang* + + 15. **Did You Know (3)**, *Bert Guiang* + + 16. **Did You Know (4)**, *Bert Guiang* + + 17. **Did You Know (5)**, *Bert Guiang* + + 18. **Sharing Trivia**, *Bert Guiang* + +

Writings 4A Book, 2012 + + 1. **The State of Our Nation and Democracy In 2010: Building 'The Good Society" We Want**, *Dr. Jose V. Abueva* + + 2. **Assessing the Expanded Role of AFP in Nation Building**, *Col. Dencio (Dennis) Acop, Ret,* + + 3. **Assessing RP's Security Strategies, Alternative Views**, *Col. Dencio (Dennis) Acop, Ret.* + 4. **The Way We Were**, *Fred Natividad* + + 5. **Veterans of Ipo Dam, A Fiction**, *Fred Natividad* + + 6. **A Plea**, *Miguel Reyes Reynaldo* + + 7. **International Youth Bowling, My Impressions**, *Marjorie Ann Elizes Reyes* +

Writings 4B Book, 2012 + + 1. **Mi Ultimo Adios (My Last Farewell)**, *Dr. Jose P. Rizal* + + 2. **Aling Pagibig Sa Tinubuang Bayan**, *Gat. Andres Bonifacio* + + 3. **Rekonsilasyun Dula (Reunion in Heaven)**, *A Play, Irineo P. Goce (KaPule2 or Leonidas P. Agbayani)* + + 4. **Forgery of Rizal Retraction**, *Irineo P. Goce (KaPule2 or Leonidas P. Agbayani)* + + 5. **Maikling Kasaysayan Ng Malas Na Bayang Pilipinas**, *Ireneo P. Goce (KaPule2 or Leonidas P. Agbayani)*

Writings 5 Book - "Best Hopes" 2010 (About President P-Noy) + I. **The Challenge of a Hundred Days: Believing that Filipinos can...** - *Tony Meloto* + II. **The 2006 Ramon Magsaysay Award for Community Service** - *for Tony Meloto* + III. **Open Letter to Noynoy** - *F. Sionil Jose, famous writer/auhor* + IV. **A History of Pain** - *Juan L. Mercado, Journalist* + V. **An Open Letter to Noynoy** - *From OFWS* + VI. **Pursuit of Good Governance Advocacies** - *Marcelo Tecson, Financial Expert* + VII. **A Fervent Prayer for Peace** - *Cesar Torres, Academcian, UP Professor* + VIII. **A History of Betrayal** - *Perry Diaz, Columnist* + IX. **Corona's Thorny Crown** - *Perry Diaz. Columnist* + X. **Dawn of a New Era** - *Perry Diaz, Columnist* + XI. **Of Mice, Boys and Men** - *Philip S. Chua, MD* + XII. **A Hopeful Tomorrow - A Balikbayan Insight** - *Philip S. Chua, MD* + XIII. **Global Filipinos: A Sleeping Giant** - *Philip S. Chua, MD* + XIV. **Heart to Heart - Winds of Change** - *Philip S. Chua, MD* + XV. **Growing Old is a Privilege** - *Philip S. Chua, MD* + XVI. **Our Cruelty to Mother Earth** - *Philip S. Chua, MD* + XVII. **Advice to Grads: "Never Choose Your Heroes Lightly"** - *Ernie Delfin, writer* + XVIII. **Gawad Kalinga, A Progressive Movement** - *Ernie Delfin, write* + XIX. **Why a Man Must Save and Invest** - *Ernie Delfin, writer* + XX. **Beautiful San Francisco, Pinoy Heaven** - *Ted Laguatan, lawyer, writer* + XXI. **The next President and PAMUSA** - *Frank Wenceslao, Pamusa President* + XXII. **Philippne Budget Deficit** - *Frank Weneslao, Pamusa President* + XXIII. **Money Laundering: US Tools vs. Corruption** - *Frank Wenceslao, Pamusa* + XXIV. **Amid the Fighting, Clan Rules Maguindanao** - *Jaileen F. Jimeno, joumalist* + XXV. **Why I Publish Writings** - *Tatay Jobo Elizes, POD Publisher*

Timeless Writings-15 (TW15), 2014 + + 1. Protecting the Nation's Marine Wealth in the West Philippine Sea, *SC Justice Antonio T. Carpio* + + 2. Are Filipinos United Against China's Invasion of Ayungin Shoal, *Rodel Rodis* + + 3. Telltale Signs: Why are there So Many Nurses in the US?, *Rodel Rodis* + + 4. Telltale Signs: Philippines - A Jewish Refugee from the Holocaust, *Rodel Rodis* + + 5. Telltale Signs: OFW Remittances Promote Mendicant Culture, *Rodel Rodis* + + 6. Adding Insult to Injury: UP College Named After Marcos' Prime Minister, *Ted Laguatan* + + 7. Aguino to Nation: "This is your SONA", *Pres. Benigno Aquino III* + + 8. Why We Are Poor A Purpose for the Middle Class, *F. Sionil Jose* + + 9. Secrets of a Romantic Man, *Dr. Phil Stack* + + 10. Totoong Buhay sa Canada, *Racz Kelly* + + 11. Small Steps to Building a Nation, *Bert Armada* + + 12. The Rising of a Nation, *Bert Armada*

Solo Authored Books: + + +

Book A, **Turning Points**, *Job Elizes Sr,1968 (Reissue 2009)* + + + Book B, **Be Considerate For Once**, *Tatay Jobo Elizes (Jr), 2013* Book C, **Piglets Unlimited - Wealth**, *Tatay Jobo Elizes, 2009* + + + Book D, **Out of the Misty Sea We Must**, *Cesar Lumba, 2010* + + + Book E, **Fulfilled** – *Gonzales Reynaldo, Editor, 2010* + + + Book F - **Reflections** - *Bert Guiang, 2010* + + + Book G, **Writings 7 - My Vintage Pics**, *Tatay Jobo Elizes, 2010* + Book H, **May Bagwis Ang Pag-ibig**, *Percival C. Cruz* + + + Book I, **Letters To Matrimony**, *Irineo P. Goce, Ka Pule2, 2011* + Book J, **Songs I Wish You Knew**, *Soledad R. Juan, 2011* + + + Book K, **Make My Day**, *Larry Henares Jr., 1993, Re-issue 2011* + Book L, **Our Guerrero Family**, *Tatay Jobo Elizes, 2010* + + + Book M, **Handy Jokes**, *Tatay J. Elizes, 2011* + Book N, **FaveArt 1**, *Tatay Jobo Elizes, 2011* + + Book O, **Beyond idle thoughts**, *MLMunoz, Sept,2011* + + + Book P, **Cracks In The Armor**, *Mariano Ngan, Oct 2011* + + + Book Q, **FaveArt 2**, *Tatay Jobo Elizes, 2011* + + Book R, **Balitang Kutsero**, *Perry Diaz, Jan 2012* + + + Book S, **FaveArt3**, *Tatay Jobo, 2011* + + + Book T, **FaveArt4**, *2012, Tatay Jobo* + + + Book U, **Stack Family Journals**, *Phil & Fe Stack, 2012* + + + Book V, **Emily, An Adoption Journey**, *Romerl Elizes, 2012* + + + Book W, **Hermes Alegre Art Gallery**, *TJ & Hermes, 2012* + + + Book X, **Masaya Din, Malungkot Din**, *Jovelyn B. Revilla, 2012* Book Y, **Tiis, Sipag At Tiyaga**, *Raquel Delfin Padilla, 2012* + + + Book Z, **Until I Meet You**, *Jhackie Eslit Bayobay, 2012* + + + Book AA, **Buhay At Pag-ibig**, *Argel Lucero Tamayo, 2012* + + + Book AB, **Hail to the Second Best**, *Dr. Philip Stack, 2012* + + + Book AC, **Life Bus**, *Mommy Joyce Pineda-Faulmino, 2012* + + + Book AD, **My Candid Musings**, *Monette Dioquino Calugay, 2012* + Book AE, **Tickets to Life**, *Maria Lourdes Jesalva, 2012* + + + Book AF, **The Dove Files**, *Mike Portes, 2012* + + + Book AG, **Nursing Vignettes**, *Jocelyn Cerrudo Sese, 2012* + Book AH, **Poor Ba Us**, *R.A. Gubalane, 2012* + + + Book AI, **Summer Idyll**, *Avelina Gil, 2012* + + Book AJ, **Legacy (Pamana)**, *Rachel Astrero, 2012* + + Book AK, **Narratives Old & New**, *Avelina J. Gil, 2013* + + Book AL, **Buhay Saudi**, *Adele J. Esic, 2013* + + Book AM, **Buhay Ofw Atbp**, *Jessica Napat, 2013* + + Book AN, **Mga Tula Ng Buhay**, *Angelita C. Esguerra, 2013* + + Book AO, **Not by Bread Alone**, *Judge Lily V. Magtolis, 2013* + + Book AP, **Jokes Collection-2**, *Tatay Jobo Elizes, 2013* + + + Book AR, *My Writings Sometimes, Tatay Jobo Elizes, 2013* + + Book AS, **Sa 'Yo Na Ako**, *Shayne A. Martinez, 2013* + + Book AT, **My Kin's Family Trees**, *Tatay Jobo Elizes, 2013* + + Book AU, **Rizal Family Tree & Others**, *Tatay Jobo Elizes, 2013* + + Book AV, **Make My Day-2, Nice & Nasty**, *L. Henares, 2013 (1993)* + + Book AW, **Make My Day-3, Cecilia, Love**, *L.Henares, 2013 (1993)*Book AX, **Handy Lyrics-1**, *Tatay Jobo Elizes, 2013* + + Book AY, **Ang Biblos**, *Rev. Dr. Eugenio Guerrero, 2014 (1929)* + + Book AZ, **Make My Day-4, *Sweet & Sour*, *L. Henares, 2014 (1993)* + + Book BA, **Life's Journey, True Stories**, *Dr. Phil Stack, 2014* + + Book BB, **Gerry Gil Writings, 2014**, *Danny Gil* + + Book BC, **Mr. President**, *Hermie Rotea, 2014* + + Book BD, **Nostalgic Pics 1**, *Tatay Jobo Elizes, 2014* + + Book BE, **MakeMyDay-5, Saints & Sinners**, *Henares, 2014 (1993)* + + Book BF, **MakeMyDay-6, Villains & Heroes**, *Henares, 2014 (1993)* + + Book BG, **Nostalgic Pics 2 (ElizesClan)**, *TatayJE, 2014* + + Book BH, **MakeMyDay-7, Tough & Tender**, *Henares, 2014(1993)* + + Book BI, **MakeMyDay-8, Light & Shadow**, *Henares, 2014(1993)* + + Book BJ, **MakeMyDay-9, Give & Take**, *Henares, 2014(1993)* + + Book BK, **MakeMyDay-10, ToBeOrNotToBe**, *Henares, 2014(1993)* + Book BL,**Emily Forever In Love, Poems,***Emily Espanol Derry, 2013* + + Book BM, **The Sinatra Songbook**, *Henares, 2014* + + Book BN, **The Gaborro Reader**, *Allen Gaborro, 2010*

Publisher: Tatay Jobo Elizes was born in Manila, Philippines, in 1934, retiree, now based in NY, busy self-publishing and involved in piglets dispersal programs in Philippines.
Acknowledgement & Dedication: Gratitude and acknowledgment belongs to those who support my hobby publishing books and charities. I heartily dedicate this to my wife, **Cora**, my children, **Tetchie, Chevy & Abeth, and Marie & Bimbo**, my grandchildren, **Karines & Aung, Noelle, Chad, Marjo, Jeb, Marvin & Marty**, great-grandson **Jason Win** and my siblings **Susan, Hilda, Bobby, Bey & Manny** and to all my extended relatives.
ISBN Code. Printed in the United States of America under ISBN code below. Copies of paintings are available in the public domain.
ISBN-13: 978-1475032703 + + + ISBN-10: 1475032706

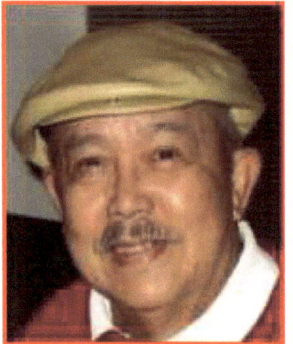

Publisher's List - Contact job_elizes@yahoo.com, tatay@usa.com
My websites: http://tinyurl.com/mj76ccq + + + www.jobelizes.com
"Buy A Book or Gift Somebody - paperback or kindle edition online"

www.ingramcontent.com/pod-product-compliance
Lightning Source LLC
Chambersburg PA
CBHW051109180526
45172CB00002B/832